St. Helens Trolleybuses

Stephen Lockwood

Series editor Robert J Harley

MP Middleton Press

**This book is dedicated to the memory of
Stanley King (1932 – 2012),
a gentleman, Bradfordian and trolleybus champion**

Published June 2013

ISBN 978 1 908174 42 0

© Middleton Press, 2013

Design Deborah Esher

Published by
        Middleton Press
        Easebourne Lane
        Midhurst
        West Sussex
        GU29 9AZ
Tel: 01730 813169
Fax: 01730 812601
Email: info@middletonpress.co.uk
www.middletonpress.co.uk

Printed in the United Kingdom by Henry Ling Limited, at the Dorset Press, Dorchester, DT1 1HD

CONTENTS

INTRODUCTION AND ACKNOWLEDGEMENTS

Following the publication of 'Trolleybus Classics' no 28 – South Lancashire Trolleybuses' in 2012, it is perhaps logical that my next volume would examine the other trolleybus operator in this area, which ran a joint service with the above company – St Helens Corporation.

Lancashire was a hot-bed of municipal bus operation and in 1950 there were 27 such undertakings in the county. However, of these only three ran trolleybuses, Manchester and Ashton under Lyne being the other two, although there was also the company owned South Lancashire Transport system.

The St Helens system was of medium size, at its peak running a fleet of 65 vehicles over 20 miles of route, plus the 10 miles owned by South Lancashire Transport Company between Haydock and Atherton. Like this Company, many of the vehicles (in fact all the vehicles built up to 1945) were of lowbridge construction (see Glossary) to enable operation under restricted height bridges.

This album takes the reader on a trolleybus ride over the routes, showing how the town and its trolleybuses looked in the years between the 1920s and the 1950s. Two books have previously been published as historical works, these being: 'Local Transport in St Helens 1879 to 1974' by M Ashton and TB Maund (1995), and 'St Helens Trolleybuses' by G Sandford (2003). Readers requiring a detailed historical background are referred to these publications.

The abandonment as early as February 1952 of all the town trolleybus routes (except the Parr route) has caused problems in the provision of suitable photographic coverage. Such images hardly seem to exist of these sections. Were it not for local photographer Norman Forbes, there may have been no coverage of these routes at all. Happily, pictorial coverage of trolleybus operation in the closing years of the system is much more plentiful.

As ever, this album could not have been created without the help of many friends who have so willingly given their support. Foremost is Geoff Sandford, author of the book mentioned above, who has been very forthcoming supplying photographs and information. Geoff, together with Phillip Taylor and Jim Saunders has also read through my text and suggested improvements and clarifications. The route maps have been drawn by Roger Smith, and are based on one originally drawn by him for Bruce Maund. Eric Old has supplied tickets, and the timetable extracts come from the collection of Colin Wright. The scale drawing of a 'Johannesburg' type trolleybus has been specially drawn for this book by Terry Russell. The following have answered my request for photographs :- Peter Caunt, John Fozard, David Hall of the British Trolleybus Society, Chris Heaps, Martin Jenkins of the Online Transport Archive, Don Jones, the late Stanley King, Bruce Maund, Alan Oxley of the Omnibus Society, Douglas Parker, Hugh Taylor, Phillip Taylor, Paul Watson and Colin Wright. Thanks go to all.

Readers will note that this volume is dedicated to the memory of Stanley King, who died suddenly in October 2012. I had known Stanley for almost fifty years, and he was always willing to lend his support to books such as this. Many of his photographs appear in this album, these being loaned to me by Stanley at what sadly was to be our last meeting together. It is fitting that the St Helens trolleybus system was one of his favourites, and as a Bradfordian, he was able to enjoy some of the vehicles long after they ceased to run in St Helens.

My last mention of thanks goes to my wife Eileen, who has the critical role of checking my text from its initial version to the final printer's proofs.

Photograpic credits

Except where noted -
Photographs credited to R. (Roy) Brook are courtesy of Paul Watson.
Photographs credited to D.A.Jones are courtesy of the
London Trolleybus Preservation Society.

Timetable extracts

The timetable extracts inserted throughout the book show details of the main services operated in June 1948.

Abbreviations and glossary

SLT	The South Lancashire Transport Company – trolleybus operator.
BUT	British United Traction – trolleybus chassis manufacturer.
BICC	British Insulated Callender's Cables – trolleybus overhead equipment manufacturer based at Prescot.
Lowbridge	A type of bus bodywork construction that produced a body lower than a conventional bus body, enabling operation under some low bridges. This was achieved by having a sunken gangway on the upper deck, with seats arranged in long benches. The sunken gangway intruded into the lower saloon, reducing the headroom for passengers on one side. On a trolleybus the height of such a vehicle was about 14 feet.
Highbridge	Trolleybuses with conventional seating on the upper deck, had a height of around 15 feet.

GEOGRAPHICAL AND HISTORICAL SETTING

Situated about 10 miles north east from Liverpool, St Helens is a medium sized industrial town which is part of the Merseyside conurbation. In trolleybus days the town was in Lancashire and the population in 1950 was around 95,000. The main industries were mining, pharmaceuticals, (the town was the home of Beecham's Pills), and glass making (eg Ravenhead and Pilkington). The latter concern is still a big employer in the town. The Corporation Transport undertaking was absorbed into the Merseyside Passenger Transport Authority in 1974. To the south west of the town lies Rainhill railway station, one of the world's historic railway sites. The famous locomotive trials took place here in 1829 just prior to the opening of the Liverpool and Manchester Railway. This skirted the south of the town and there was also a station on this line at St Helens Junction. Both stations were served by the trolleybuses.

HISTORICAL BACKGROUND

Powers to operate trolleybuses (and motorbuses) by St Helens Corporation were included in the St Helens Corporation Act, 1921. Until 1919, the town's tramway system, although municipally owned, had been leased and operated by the New St Helens and District Tramways Company. In that year the Corporation took over the running of the system which required considerable investment, not least the condition of the track.

One of the worst stretches of track was on the Prescot via Rainhill route, particularly on the A57 road between Rainhill and Prescot. As required by the above Act of Parliament, a Provisional Order to run trolleybuses on the section of route between Toll Bar and Prescot (via Rainhill) was applied for in 1923, and this was granted in the following year. However, for financial reasons the Corporation was not able to take any further action until 1926, when an order for four Garrett single deck trolleybuses was placed, for operation between Rainhill (Mental Hospital Gates) to Prescot. The portion of tram route between Toll Bar and Rainhill Hospital would remain tram operated because of heavy loadings. The tram service beyond the latter point to Prescot was replaced temporarily by motorbuses in March 1927 to allow reconstruction of the A57 road and the overhead. The trolleybus overhead equipment was supplied by British Insulated Cables Ltd, whose works were on the line of route near Prescot. Immediately following the Ministry of Transport inspection, the trolleybus route was opened on 11th July 1927. Through passengers needed to change from tram to trolleybuses (and vice-versa), and through tickets were issued. The Garrett trolleybuses were required to gain access to and from the town centre depot by taking power from the single tram positive wire, and trailing a skate in the tram track along the tram route to Rainhill. This was some considerable distance, being over two miles, and it is recorded that they carried passengers on this section. At Prescot, the trolleybuses met the St Helens trams running via the direct route via Portico and Eccleston Lane Ends, as well as Liverpool Corporation trams.

The trolleybuses were deemed a success and well liked by the public, even though the arrangements at Rainhill Hospital described above were not ideal.

Plans were now progressed to convert other tram routes, and on 30th July 1929, trolleybuses were introduced on the Parr route to the south east of the town. This introduced trolleybuses to the town centre, and as a result four Ransomes single deckers entered service, joining a single Ransomes vehicle obtained in 1928 to augment the Garretts. The Parr route was extended from the tram terminus at the 'Horse Shoe' along Derbyshire Hill Road to Fleet Lane.

The next route to be converted, on 21st June 1931, was that from the town to Haydock where the new trolleybus wiring met that of the SLT, thus completing the long 14 mile through route to Atherton, jointly operated by the Corporation and the SLT company. The SLT trams between Atherton and Ashton in Makerfield had been replaced by trolleybuses in the previous year, and during this period St Helens maintained the tram service from the St Helens direction to Ashton, beyond the boundary at Haydock. This arrangement was due to the construction of the East Lancashire Road (A580) which crossed the route by an overbridge between Haydock and Ashton. Five double-deck six-wheel lowbridge bodied Ransomes trolleybuses were provided to operate St Helens contribution of the service.

The success of trolleybus operation meant the plans were now laid to convert the remaining tram routes. The Windle City route was opened to trolleybuses on 16th May 1934, the route being extended to Moss Bank (crossing the East Lancashire Road on the level). A short-working reversing triangle was provided at the former tram terminus at Hard Lane. The Rainhill trams succumbed on 3rd July 1934, and the original trolleybus service from there to Prescot was duly extended into the town centre, eliminating the change of vehicle for through passengers. 1st May 1935 saw the St Helens Junction route change to trolleybuses, followed later that month, on the 29th, by the Denton's Green service. The only tram route remaining was the direct service to Prescot via Portico, and St Helens' last tram operated on this route on 31st March 1936. The replacing trolleybuses operated a circular service to Prescot, ie out via Portico, returning via Rainhill and vice-versa. To run all these routes, 29 four-wheel double deckers with lowbridge bodies entered

continued ...

ST. HELENS
CORPORATION TRANSPORT
Trolleybus Wiring
Map 1

N
W · E
S

Scale exaggerated at junctions
and turning circles.

| 0 | 0,5 | 1,0 kilometre |

| 0 | ¼ | ½ | ¾ | 1 mile |

| 0 | 500 | 1000 yards |

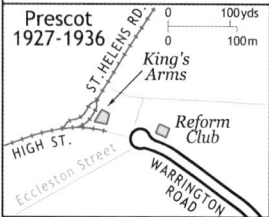

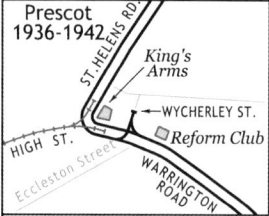

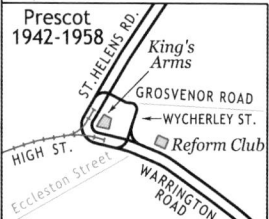

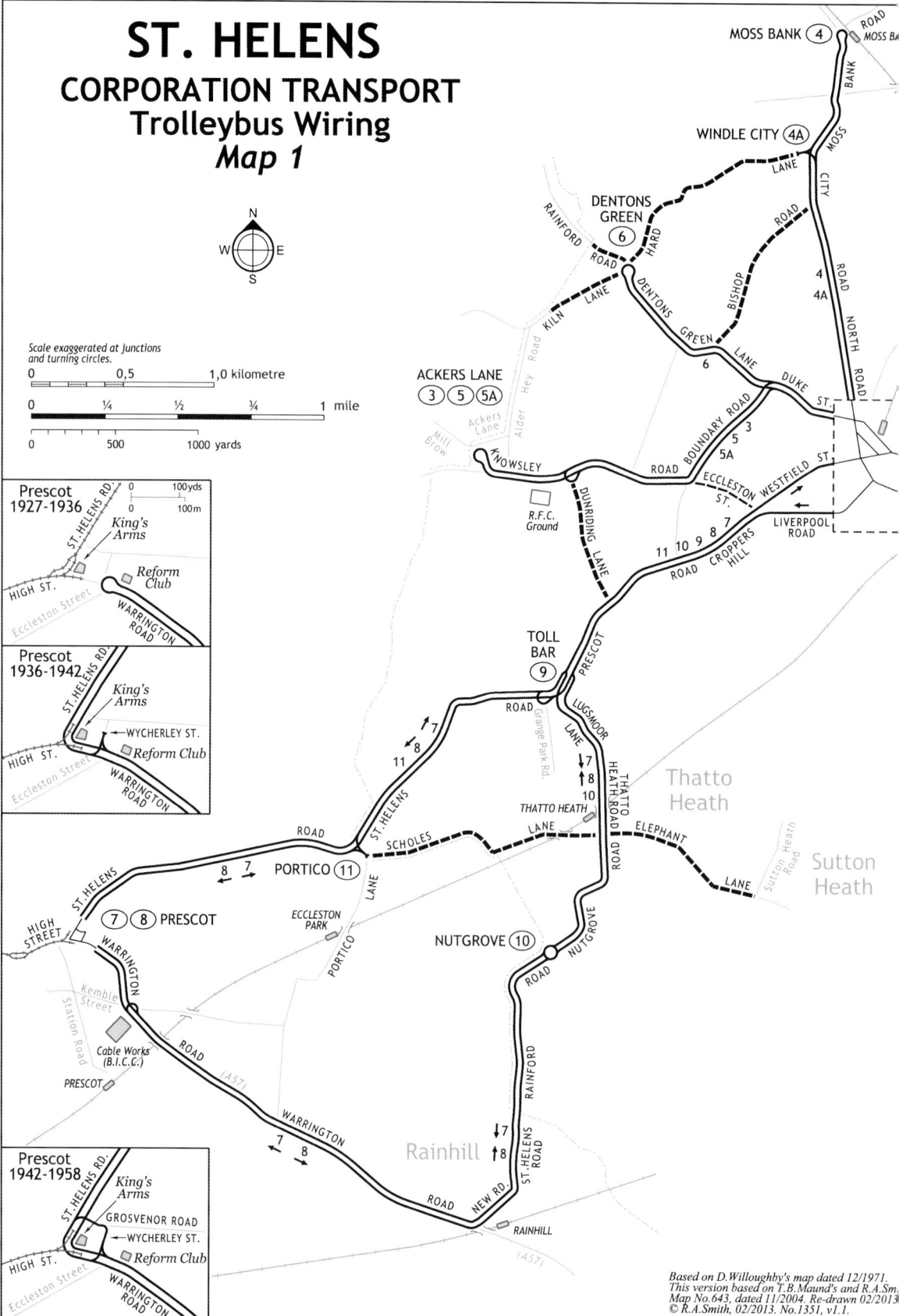

MOSS BANK (4)

ROAD
MOSS BA

MOSS BANK

WINDLE CITY (4A)

CITY

LANE

ROAD

NORTH ROAD

4
4A

DENTONS
GREEN (6)

RAINFORD ROAD

HARD

DENTONS GREEN LANE

BISHOP

ROAD

KILN LANE

Alder Hey Road

6

DUKE ST.

ACKERS LANE
(3) (5) (5A)

Ackers
Lane

HILL
BROW

KNOWSLEY

BOUNDARY ROAD

3
5
5A

ECCLESTON
ST.

WESTFIELD ST.

ROAD

LIVERPOOL
ROAD

R.F.C.
Ground

DUNRIDING LANE

8
7

11 10 9

ROAD CROPPERS HILL

Prescot
1927-1936

| 0 | 100 yds |
| 0 | 100m |

ST.HELENS RD.

King's
Arms

Reform
Club

HIGH ST.

Eccleston Street

WARRINGTON ROAD

Prescot
1936-1942

ST.HELENS RD.

King's
Arms

WYCHERLEY ST.

Reform Club

HIGH ST.

Eccleston Street

WARRINGTON ROAD

TOLL
BAR (9)

PRESCOT

LUGSMOOR LANE

THATTO HEATH ROAD

Thatto
Heath

7
8
11

ROAD

Grange Park Rd.

7
8
10

THATTO HEATH

LANE

ELEPHANT

Sutton Heath Road

Sutton
Heath

ST.HELENS

SCHOLES LANE

LANE

ROAD

LANE

ROAD

8   7
PORTICO (11)

PORTICO LANE

ECCLESTON
PARK

NUTGROVE (10)

NUTGROVE ROAD

ST.HELENS

(7) (8) PRESCOT

WARRINGTON

RAINFORD ROAD

HIGH
STREET

Kemble
Street

Station Road

Cable Works
(B.I.C.C.)

ROAD

PRESCOT

ROAD (A57)

WARRINGTON

7   8

ROAD

NEW RD.

ST.HELENS ROAD

7
8

Rainhill

RAINHILL

(A57)

Prescot
1942-1958

ST.HELENS RD.

King's
Arms

GROSVENOR ROAD

WYCHERLEY ST.

Reform Club

HIGH ST.

Eccleston Street

WARRINGTON ROAD

Based on D.Willoughby's map dated 12/1971.
This version based on T.B.Maund's and R.A.Sm
Map No.643, dated 11/2004. Re-drawn 02/201
© R.A.Smith, 02/2013. No.1351, v1.1.

East Lancashire Road (A580)

East Lancashire Road

Piele Road

Haydock

Huntsman Hotel

VICARAGE RD.

WEST END ROAD

CLIPSLEY

1 2 3

L.C.

CHURCH ROAD

HAYDOCK LANE

Haydock Colliery

Ship Inn

WEST

BLACK-BROOK RD.

(3A) BLACKBROOK

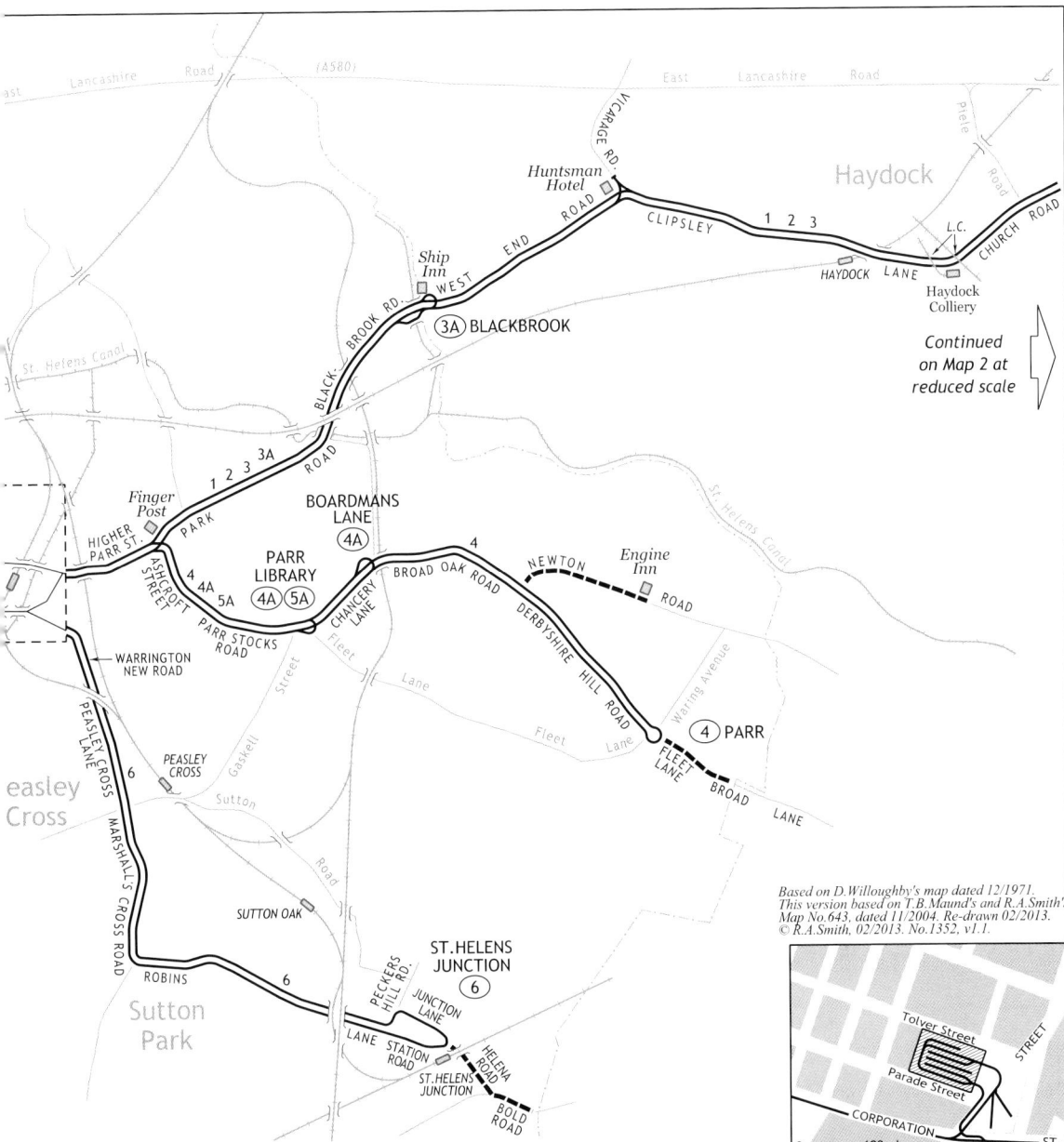

Continued on Map 2 at reduced scale

St. Helens Canal

BLACK-BROOK ROAD

1 2 3 3A

Finger Post

BOARDMANS LANE

(4A)

St. Helens Canal

HIGHER PARR ST.

PARK

ASHCROFT STREET

PARR LIBRARY

(4A) (5A)

4 4A 5A

CHANCERY LANE

BROAD OAK ROAD

4

NEWTON ROAD

Engine Inn

PARR STOCKS ROAD

Fleet Street

Lane

DERBYSHIRE HILL ROAD

Waring Avenue

(4) PARR

WARRINGTON NEW ROAD

Gaskell Street

Fleet Lane

FLEET LANE

BROAD LANE

PEASLEY CROSS LANE

PEASLEY CROSS

Sutton Road

easley Cross

MARSHALL'S CROSS ROAD

6

SUTTON OAK

Based on D.Willoughby's map dated 12/1971.
This version based on T.B.Maund's and R.A.Smith's Map No.643, dated 11/2004. Re-drawn 02/2013.
© R.A.Smith, 02/2013. No.1352, v1.1.

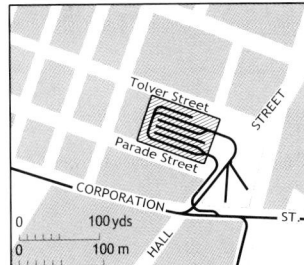

ROBINS

6

Sutton Park

PECKERS HILL RD.

ST.HELENS JUNCTION

(6)

JUNCTION LANE

LANE STATION ROAD

ST.HELENS JUNCTION

HELENA ROAD

BOLD ROAD

Tolver Street

STREET

Parade Street

CORPORATION ST.

HALL STREET

0   100 yds
0   100 m

Legend

	St. Helens Corporation trolleybus wiring as in February 1952
	S.L.T. wiring used by St. Helens Corporation
	other S.L.T. wiring
(3) 3	terminus and service number
▬ ▬ ▬	trolleybus route authorised but not built
┼┼┼	tramway
	other roads
	St. Helens borough boundary
▭	main line railway and station
┼┼┼	industrial railway
	canal

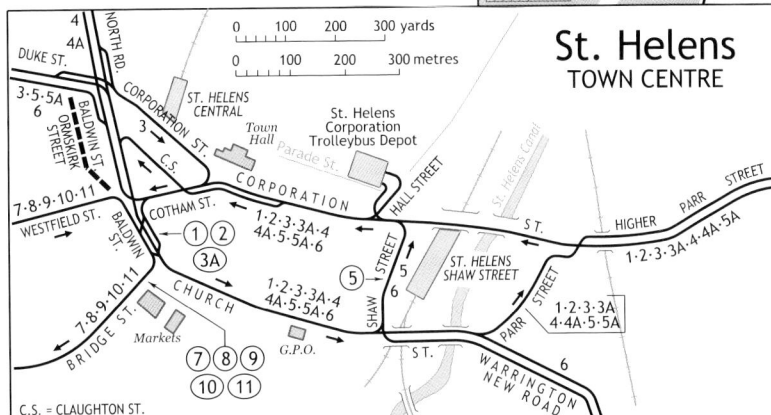

St. Helens
TOWN CENTRE

4
4A

DUKE ST.

NORTH RD.

CORPORATION ST.

ST. HELENS CENTRAL

3·5·5A 6

BALDWIN ST.

ORMSKIRK STREET

3

Town Hall

Parade St.

St. Helens Corporation Trolleybus Depot

St. Helens Canal

0   100   200   300 yards
0   100   200   300 metres

C.S.

CORPORATION ST.

HALL STREET

PARR STREET

7·8·9·10·11

WESTFIELD ST.

COTHAM ST.

1·2·3·3A·4 4A·5·5A·6

HIGHER PARR ST.

1·2·3·3A·4·4A·5A

(1) (2)

(3A)

BALDWIN ST.

(5)

SHAW STREET

5

ST. HELENS SHAW STREET

7·8·9·10·11

CHURCH ST.

1·2·3·3A·4 4A·5·5A·6

5 6

1·2·3·3A 4·4A·5·5A

BRIDGE ST.

Markets

G.P.O.

PARR ST.

6

(7) (8) (9)

(10) (11)

WARRINGTON NEW ROAD

C.S. = CLAUGHTON ST.

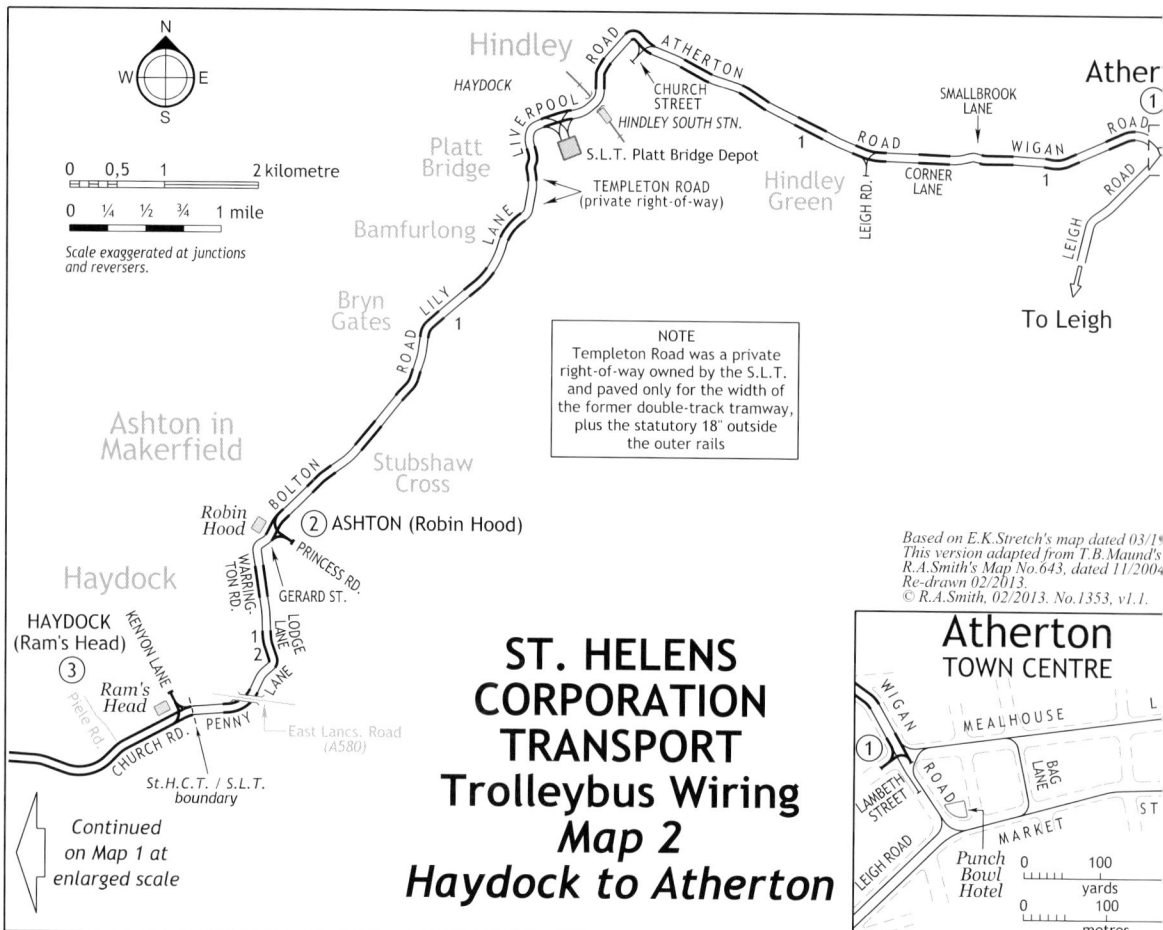

ST. HELENS
CORPORATION
TRANSPORT
Trolleybus Wiring
Map 2
Haydock to Atherton

Based on E.K.Stretch's map dated 03/1■
This version adapted from T.B.Maund's
R.A.Smith's Map No.643, dated 11/200■
Re-drawn 02/2013.
© R.A.Smith, 02/2013. No.1353, v1.1.

NOTE
Templeton Road was a private
right-of-way owned by the S.L.T.
and paved only for the width of
the former double-track tramway,
plus the statutory 18" outside
the outer rails

Scale exaggerated at junctions
and reversers.

Continued
on Map 1 at
enlarged scale

Atherton
TOWN CENTRE

... *HISTORICAL BACKGROUND* continued

service between 1934 and the end of 1936, the chassis being supplied by Leyland and Ransomes. Route mileage was now just over 19 miles, plus a further ten miles operated under SLT wires.

The fleet was bolstered in 1937-8 by a further 16 trolleybuses of Leyland or Ransomes types, these being used partly to replace the ageing single-deckers.

In 1942, in the midst of wartime, St Helens was allocated ten new trolleybuses. These were based on Sunbeam four-wheel chassis built for export to Johannesburg. Lowbridge bodies were provided to wartime utility specification. These vehicles were 8-feet wide, not a legal size for British operation, and special dispensation had to be given by the Ministry of Transport. On 29th June 1943, the Eccleston bus service was taken over by trolleybuses to save vehicles and fuel. This route was a branch off the Denton's Green service and terminated at Ackers Lane. It also served the St Helens Rugby League ground at Dunriding Lane, and a short working turning loop was provided to allow extra journeys to operate on match days. Just after the cessation of the war, at the end of 1945, a further ten 'utility' bodied vehicles entered service.

In the immediate post-war years, the trolleybus system had a seemingly bright future. Many existing vehicles were being rebuilt or rebodied, and 16 brand new vehicles were ordered for delivery at the turn of the decade. Several route extensions were planned, these being detailed in the St Helens Corporation Act of 1942. In 1947 the fleet comprised 62 vehicles, all double deck four wheel lowbridge type.

The following routes were in operation in June 1948:-

1	Atherton – St Helens (joint with SLT)
2	Ashton in Makerfield - St Helens
3	Ackers Lane - Haydock (Rams Head)
3A	Ackers Lane - Blackbrook
4	Moss Bank – Parr via town centre
5	Ackers Lane – town centre (Baldwin Street)
5A	Ackers Lane - Parr Library
6	Denton's Green – St Helens Junction
7	St Helens – Rainhill - Prescot, returning via Portico
8	St Helens – Portico – Prescot, returning via Rainhill
9	St Helens – Toll Bar
10	St Helens – Rainhill Hospital
11	St Helens - Portico

Note – service numbers were introduced during wartime. Services 9 to 11 were short workings of the Prescot route, and the numbers varied over the years – eg by the mid-1950s extra journeys turning at Prescot and not operating as a circular were numbered 9.

The new trolleybuses were delivered between 1950 and 1951, and were of highbridge construction. This meant that they could not operate to St Helens Junction or to Atherton due to low bridges, and in the case of the former route the new General Manager, R Edgley Cox, devised an ingenious warning device to prevent the new vehicles accidentally trying to pass under the bridge. Apart from one day in 1956 to be depicted later, the post-war vehicles spent their entire lives on the Prescot services.

Contrary to expectations, a review of municipal transport provision in the town concluded that all the trolleybus services except those to Parr, Prescot and Atherton should be replaced by motorbuses, which would then operate extended routes into new areas. This cull occurred after operation on 2nd February 1952. At that time a new short working turning point was provided on the Parr route at Boardman's Lane, which became peak hour service 4A, replacing the journeys to Parr Library. The fleet was reduced to 40 vehicles and all the wiring in the town centre north of Coatham Street (except for a one-way loop via Claughton Street – Baldwin Street – Sefton Place, allowing the Parr trolleybuses to turn round) was removed.

In mid-1955, all the surviving members of the fleet had their fleet numbers increased by 200, ie no 101 became no. 301. This affected pre-war Leylands numbered from 101-104, the wartime utility trolleybuses, and the post war vehicles. The Parr service was largely replaced by motorbuses after 12th November 1955, although the peak hour 4A service survived, and the retention of the wiring to Parr terminus meant that trolleybuses occasionally ran isolated journeys on the full route in emergencies. Besides the 4A service, the only other trolleybus service operating entirely within the town boundary was service 3 to Haydock (together with the 3A short working to Blackbrook).

The run-down of the trolleybus system continued in 1956 when the Atherton and Haydock services were changed to motorbuses after 11th November. The 4A Boardman's Lane service was abandoned at the same time (the last journeys being on 9th November). This left the busy Prescot services 7 and 8, which had been mainly operated by the new post war vehicles since their delivery at the start of the decade. These routes operated until 30th June 1958, and a final farewell journey was taken by civic representatives on the following day. All the post war vehicles were sold for further service, the eight Sunbeams going to South Shields and the eight BUTs going to Bradford, where two survived in service into the 1970s.

ST HELENS CORPORATION TRANSPORT
Chronology of Trolleybus Routes 1927 - 1958

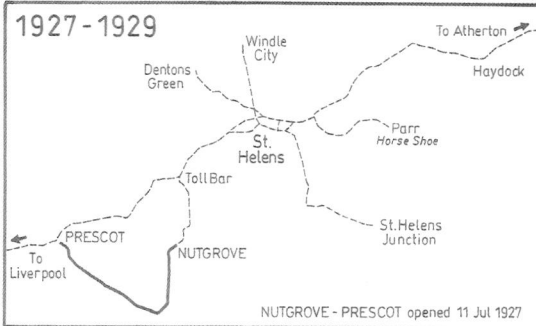

1927 - 1929

Windle City · To Atherton · Haydock · Dentons Green · Parr Horse Shoe · St. Helens · Toll Bar · St. Helens Junction · PRESCOT · To Liverpool · NUTGROVE

NUTGROVE - PRESCOT opened 11 Jul 1927

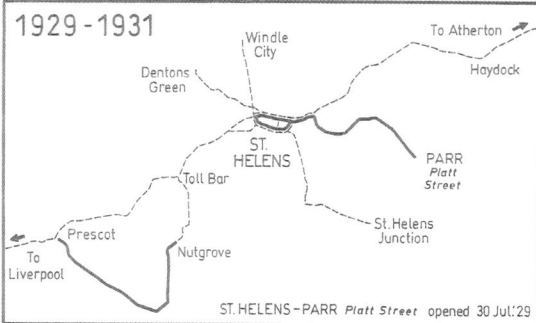

1929 - 1931

Windle City · To Atherton · Haydock · Dentons Green · ST. HELENS · PARR Platt Street · Toll Bar · St. Helens Junction · Prescot · To Liverpool · Nutgrove

ST. HELENS - PARR Platt Street opened 30 Jul '29

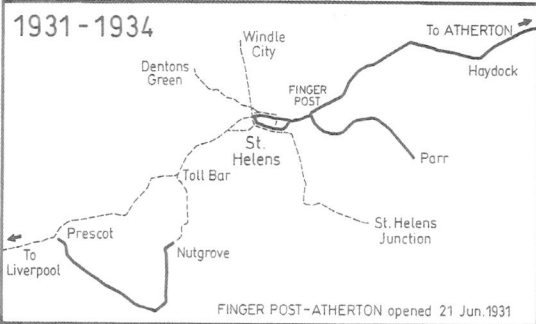

1931 - 1934

Windle City · To ATHERTON · Haydock · Dentons Green · FINGER POST · St. Helens · Parr · Toll Bar · St. Helens Junction · Prescot · To Liverpool · Nutgrove

FINGER POST - ATHERTON opened 21 Jun. 1931

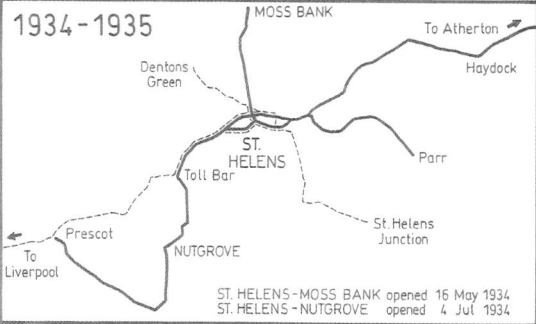

1934 - 1935

MOSS BANK · To Atherton · Haydock · Dentons Green · ST. HELENS · Parr · Toll Bar · St. Helens Junction · Prescot · To Liverpool · NUTGROVE

ST. HELENS - MOSS BANK opened 16 May 1934
ST. HELENS - NUTGROVE opened 4 Jul 1934

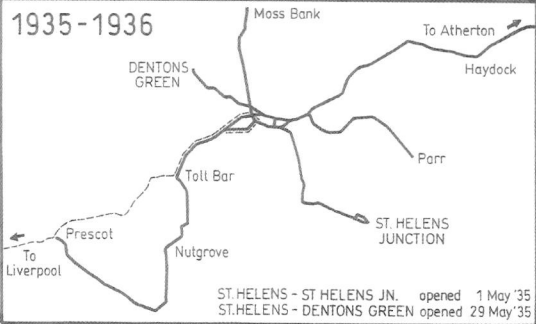

1935 - 1936

Moss Bank · To Atherton · Haydock · DENTONS GREEN · Parr · Toll Bar · ST. HELENS JUNCTION · Prescot · To Liverpool · Nutgrove

ST. HELENS - ST HELENS JN. opened 1 May '35
ST. HELENS - DENTONS GREEN opened 29 May '35

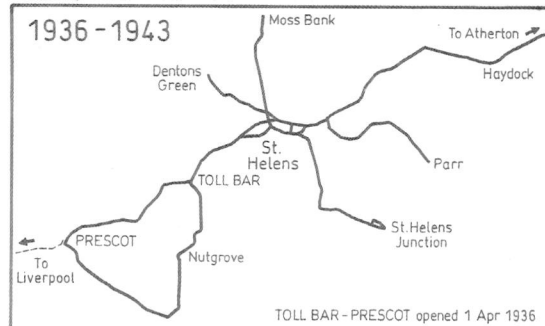

1936 - 1943

Moss Bank · To Atherton · Haydock · Dentons Green · St. Helens · Parr · TOLL BAR · St. Helens Junction · PRESCOT · To Liverpool · Nutgrove

TOLL BAR - PRESCOT opened 1 Apr 1936

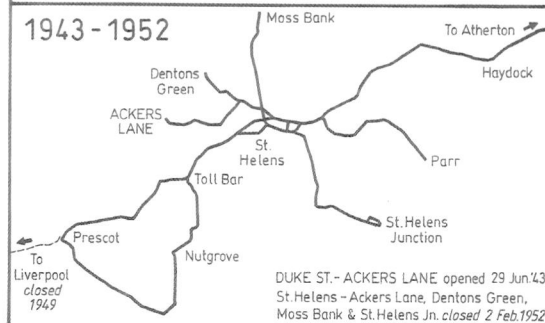

1943 - 1952

Moss Bank · To Atherton · Haydock · Dentons Green · ACKERS LANE · St. Helens · Parr · Toll Bar · St. Helens Junction · Prescot · To Liverpool closed 1949 · Nutgrove

DUKE ST. - ACKERS LANE opened 29 Jun '43
St.Helens - Ackers Lane, Dentons Green, Moss Bank & St.Helens Jn. closed 2 Feb.1952

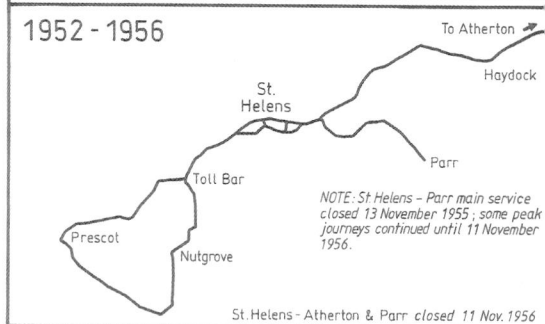

1952 - 1956

To Atherton · Haydock · St. Helens · Parr · Toll Bar · Prescot · Nutgrove

NOTE: St Helens - Parr main service closed 13 November 1955; some peak journeys continued until 11 November 1956.

St.Helens - Atherton & Parr closed 11 Nov. 1956

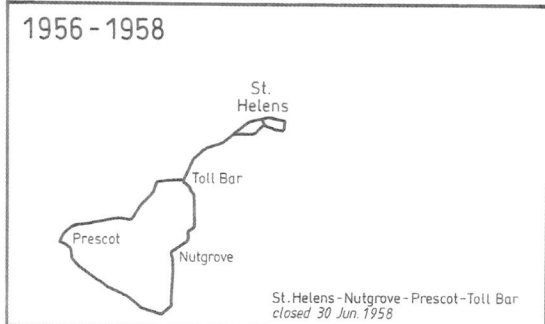

1956 - 1958

St. Helens · Toll Bar · Prescot · Nutgrove

St.Helens - Nutgrove - Prescot - Toll Bar closed 30 Jun. 1958

Legend

- - - - - tram
——— trolleybus

Scale

0 1 2 3 miles
0 1 2 3 4 5 km

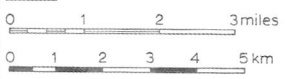
R. A. SMITH. NOV. 04. N° 644

REPLACING THE TRAMS

1.   The outer terminus of the inaugural 1927 trolleybus route was at Prescot, where Garrett no. 1 is seen outside the Reform Club. The tight turning circle within the carriageway of Warrington Road can be seen, and on the left is a Liverpool tram. A short section of track was retained here when the rails in Warrington Road were removed to allow these trams to reverse. Out of view to the left is the King's Arms junction, which was the terminus of the direct tram route to St Helens. This service would not become trolleybus operated until 1936. (British Trolleybus Society collection)

2.   This scene is at Rainhill Hospital Gates, the other terminus of the first route. Ransomes trolleybus no. 100 (formerly no. 5) is turning at the wide road junction, whilst a connecting tram stands at its terminus in Nutgrove Road. Note that the tram overhead is splayed to reach two points of the trolleybus turning circle. This allowed trolleybus crews to transfer the positive boom of their vehicle easily when travelling to or from the depot at St Helens. This point was later known as Nutgrove, and features again later in the album. (T.B.Maund collection)

3.	Trolleybuses began running in the town centre in mid-1929, when operation on the Parr route commenced. This view shows trolleybus no. 108, one of five Ransomes purchased for this route. It is standing at the town centre terminus in Ormskirk Street, together with a tram on the St Helens Junction route. Tram and trolleybus shared the overhead, so the tram cannot proceed until the trolleybus has departed. (British Trolleybus Society collection)

4.	This photograph was taken to record the completion of the conversion of the tram system to trolleybuses. On 31st March 1936 civic representatives pose beside a tram before boarding the new trolleybus for a run along the direct route to Prescot, and the creation of a circular route via Portico or Rainhill. The public trolleybus service commenced the following day. (Author's collection)

TOWN CENTRE
SEFTON PLACE

5.   This location, at the junction of Baldwin Street, Cotham Street and Ormskirk Street was at the centre of the trolleybus system, all routes passing through this point. Passengers on the Prescot route boarded at a central island, where Leyland trolleybus no. 102 is seen in this late 1930s view. More trolleybuses can be seen in the distance at the Baldwin Street, loading points for Moss Bank and Denton's Green. The wires trailing in from the right were for the Atherton and Haydock services. (J.F.Higham / A.B.Cross collection)

6.   The loading island for the Prescot routes is prominent in this pre-war view of Sefton Place looking east towards Ormskirk Street. Leyland no. 122 is the rearmost of two vehicles loading here. On the left another trolleybus is in Baldwin Street. Note the roadway paved in stone setts and evidence of the former tram track. (S.L.Smith)

7.   A close up view of the stop signs displayed at the Sefton Place terminus of the Prescot routes. (G.Sandford collection)

TRANSPORT

TROLLEY BUSES START HERE FOR

THATTO HEATH
RAINHILL
WHISTON
AND PRESCOT

TRANSPORT

TROLLEY BUSES START HERE FOR

TOLL BAR
ECCLESTON
PARK
AND
PRESCOT

TROLLEY BUS

BRIDGE STREET FOR PRESCOT

8.   Due to the blackout conditions during wartime, the island stop in Sefton Place was deemed unsafe, and the Prescot route terminus was moved to Bridge Street, outside the Market. In the 1950s, no. 375, one of the post-war Sunbeams, is seen passing the Atherton stop in Ormskirk Street on its way to Bridge Street. It is overtaking South Lancashire Transport Guy six-wheel trolleybus no. 1, new in 1930 but extensively rebuilt in 1953. (Author's collection)

9.   This broadside view is of one of the pre-war Ransomes trolleybuses with Massey bodywork. It is seen at the Prescot stand in Bridge Street outside the Market. (J.Fozard)

10.   Further along Ormskirk Street, two of the post-war Sunbeams, nos. 377 and 376, are about to turn right into Bridge Street in this busy scene, showing typical 1950s traffic. By the time of this photograph, the Prescot route would be the only trolleybus route in operation, and the wires to the left of the trolleybuses would be for depot workings only. (R.Brook)

← 11. This is a mid-1950s scene at the Market terminus of the Prescot routes. BUT no. 386 stands in front of one of the 1945 'utility' Sunbeams, providing a contrast in vehicle dimensions. The higher BUT contrasts with the lowbridge bodied Sunbeam. (R.Brook)

← 12. This photograph, taken just after the previous one, reveals that the 'utility' Sunbeam is no. 312. After the closure of the Atherton route, two of these vehicles, nos. 311 and 312, were retained for occasional use. No. 312 was the vehicle which had been experimentally fitted with trolley retrievers in 1955, and the trolley ropes can just be seen. (R.Brook)

13.   Until the delivery of the post-war vehicles, the 'Johannesburg' Sunbeams were regularly used on the Prescot route. In later years they did still appear occasionally on these routes, as evidenced by this view of no. 161 loading at the Market on an extra journey to Nutgrove for Rainhill Hospital. This vehicle was rebuilt in 1948 in Cardiff. (P.Mitchell)

AE 7713

1		34
2	7d	33
3		32
4		31
5		30
6		29
7		28
8		27
9		26
10		25
11		24
12		23
13		22
14		21
15		20
16		19
17		18

ST. HELENS CORPORATION TRANSPORT. This Ticket is available from the stage at which it is punched and must be shown or given up on demand. Not Transferable

TRANSFER

DEPOT		CHILD

← 14. The Prescot routes were the province of the post-war vehicles, and this nearside view shows BUT no. 382 beside the Market waiting to depart on route 7 to Prescot via Rainhill. The latter destination was shown around most of the route to Prescot, then it was changed to 'St Helens'; for the return journey via Portico. (R.Marshall)

15.   On leaving the Market terminal stop, Prescot trolleybuses continued on their one-way loop via Liverpool Road, joining the inbound wires at Croppers Hill (see photograph 64). This pleasant scene shows Sunbeam no. 374 about to turn into Liverpool Road. (R.Brook)

16.   On inbound journeys towards Sefton Place, trolleybuses on the Prescot circular service ran from Croppers Hill via Westfield Street. Sunbeam no. 378 is seen here passing Burchall's butchery shop, still trading in 2013. (Author's collection)

→   18. This mid-1950s view shows two of the 1945 'utility' vehicles, led by no. 306, loading at the Atherton stop, the length of the queue being typical of the demand for public transport at this time. Note the additional wiring not evident in the previous photograph – the crossings behind the vehicles allowed Prescot route vehicles coming from the depot to access the wires leading into Bridge Street. This was part of the wiring improvements in the area introduced in 1949. (R.Brook)

ORMSKIRK STREET
FOR ATHERTON

17.   Returning to Sefton Place, we now look at the Atherton route terminus (including the local Haydock service) and its exit from the town centre via Church Street. This view is dated 1948, and shows 1945 'utility' no. 111 at the Atherton stop outside the Ridings store. In the background, a trolleybus is turning from Cotham Street into Baldwin Street. Note that both vehicles are displaying the short lived streamlined 'flash' on the lower body side. (R.Marshall)

19.   St Helens and South Lancashire vehicles are seen together at the Atherton stop in mid-1956. No. 306 is operating a short-working to Ashton, numbered 2, probably in connection with a race meeting at Haydock. The South Lancashire trolleybus is no. 10, a 1930 Guy with a rebuilt front. (R.Marshall)

20.   Loading at the Atherton stop on a service 3 working to Haydock (Rams Head) is 1935 built Leyland no. 133. Its original Massey body had been replaced by an East Lancashire built one in 1944. (C.Carter)

CHURCH STREET

21.   Church Street, the town's main shopping street, was traversed by trolleybuses only in the easterly direction. 'Johannesburg' no. 158 is picking up passengers here on service 4A for Boardman's Lane. This was the new short-working point on the Parr route established in 1952. About to overtake is one of the London type 'RT' buses which replaced trolleybuses on most of the town routes in 1952. This view dates from about 1954. (D.A.Jones)

← 22. By way of contrast, this is a view at the same point, showing 'Johannesburg' no. 359 on 9th August 1955, having been newly renumbered a few months earlier. It is working the full route to Parr, which would be converted to motorbus operation three months later. (J.Copland)

← 23. Slightly further along Church Street was the stop for Atherton. Here, an SLT Guy four-wheeler pauses before resuming its 14 mile journey. The vehicle dated from 1933, and is seen in a much rebuilt state with new front end and deep side panelling. The SLT trolleybuses working on the route had to be specially licensed for operation in St Helens. (Author's collection)

24. Beyond Church Street, workings on the Parr and Atherton routes, including services to Haydock and Ashton, ran via Parr Street, joining the inbound wiring at Higher Parr Street. One of the interesting features of the system is captured here in this view in Higher Parr Street. Trolleybuses were routinely manoeuvred away from the overhead wires by means of Land Rovers fitted with a cushioned 'buffer' enabling them to push the vehicles. Here, a 1945 'utility' Sunbeam no. 108, which has been parked on the Jackson Street bus depot land (south of this point), is being propelled to reach the wires in Upper Parr Street, where it can commence service to Blackbrook. (Omnibus Society collection)

CORPORATION STREET
AND DEPOT

25.   Inbound trolleybuses from Atherton, Haydock, Parr and St Helens Junction entered the town centre by way of Corporation Street, the latter service traversing Shaw Street to reach Corporation Street. In pouring rain, 1945 'utility' Sunbeam no. 111 negotiates Corporation Street, and is opposite Hall Street, where the trolleybus depot was situated. It is working on a Haydock journey which will terminate in the town centre. (R.Marshall)

26.   Seen turning into Hall Street from Corporation Street in 1935 is new Leyland no. 127. Behind is Ransomes no. 116, the first four-wheel double decker in the fleet. (R.Marshall collection)

27.   A feature of the depot at Hall Street was the open unpaved area. Across the street from the depot building, this was wired for use as a trolleybus park. Seen in this area, known as 'the land', are two 'Johannesburg' vehicles, nos. 164 and 159. Their rebuilding after the war has resulted in detail differences to the rear emergency doors. No. 164, rebuilt by the Transport Department itself, was experimentally fitted with interior fluorescent lighting. (P.J.Taylor collection)

28.   The main works of the Transport Department were in Tolver Street, behind Hall Street depot. There was no wiring connecting the two buildings, and trolleybuses were shunted there using the Land Rovers. Leyland no. 101, with 1948 built East Lancashire body, is seen under repair at the Tolver Street premises on 17th August 1953. (C.W.Heaps)

29.　　Resuming our journey along Corporation Street, this scene is of the approach to Victoria Square. 1945 'utility' Sunbeam no. 311 has just negotiated the facing frog for the duplicated wiring. This was introduced in 1949 as part of the town centre wiring improvements. No. 311 has taken the outer wiring and will turn into Cotham Street to access the Haydock stop in Ormskirk Street. (Author's collection)

30.　　This 1935 view shows new Leyland no. 127 posed outside the Town Hall in Victoria Square, under the supervision of the constable on point duty. (R.Marshall collection)

31. The same location is seen in this early 1950s scene. South Lancashire Transport Guy six-wheeler no. 6 is passing the Town Hall and turning towards Cotham Street having almost completed a journey from Atherton. This vehicle would shortly be rebuilt with a new front. Note that the policeman is now in a high visibility white coat with extra metal protection from the traffic. (C.Carter)

32. The western end of Corporation Street was used by trolleybuses coming from Ackers Lane, Denton's Green or Moss Bank which were terminating in the town centre, to access the loading points in Baldwin Street for the return journey. It was also used, as seen here, by vehicles from Ackers Lane running through to Haydock or Blackbrook to access the stop in Ormskirk Street. In this view, 1938 Ransomes no. 138 is seen passing the west end of the Town Hall buildings, prior to turning into Cotham Street on a through journey on route 3A from Ackers Lane to Blackbrook. (P.J.Taylor collection)

COTHAM STREET AND CLAUGHTON STREET

33.   1935 built Leyland no. 133, with 1944 built East Lancashire body is in Cotham Street, prior to turning left into Ormskirk Street to start a journey to Haydock. (R.Marshall collection)

34.   The town centre wiring improvements introduced in 1949 saw new wiring erected in Claughton Street, between Cotham Street and Baldwin Street. This allowed the Parr and St Helens Junction service trolleybuses to turn in the town centre, and access the main stops for these services in Baldwin Street. This had not been possible before this date. The wiring used locally made British Insulated Callender's Cables components, a feature of which was the use of 'curve segment' assemblies on the sharp curve from Claughton Street into Baldwin Street. These considerably reduced the need for 'pull off' wires to form a curve. A close up of one of the assemblies is seen near the Baldwin Street junction. (BICC)

35.	This broad view of the curve from Claughton Street (on the left) into Baldwin Street (on the right) shows the neatness of the wiring. This and the previous photograph were used in BICC publicity. (BICC)

36.	A busy scene showing the junction of Cotham Street and Baldwin Street at Sefton Place in about 1950. Ransomes no. 143 body is seen on service 5. It has just completed a journey from Ackers Lane, and is about to return there after picking up passengers in Baldwin Street. The upstairs bench seating of the lowbridge body is evident in this view. Behind is a rebodied pre-war trolleybus on service 5A, the through service from Parr Library to Ackers Lane. (C.Carter)

BALDWIN STREET

37.　　The main town centre stops for all trolleybus services, except those to Haydock/Atherton and to Prescot, were situated in Baldwin Street. At the Moss Bank stop is 'Johannesburg' no. 165, as rebuilt after the war. Note the lettering over the cab windows – on the left 'Licence no. 73' and on the right 'To seat 50 passengers'. (R.Marshall)

38.   At the Denton's Green stop is 1935 Leyland no. 136, with 1945 built East Lancashire body. (R.Marshall)

39.   The Parr and St Helens Junction stops were at the Sefton Place end of Baldwin Street. Here, Ransomes no. 155, with Massey body is at the Parr stop. (R.Marshall)

40.   At the St Helens Junction stop is Leyland no. 135, with 1945 built East Lancashire body. Note the difference in styling between this vehicle and the East Lancashire body shown in photograph 38. (R.Marshall)

THE ROUTES

HAYDOCK AND ATHERTON

41.   After leaving the town centre via Higher Parr Street, the Haydock and Atherton routes proceeded via Park Road and Blackbrook Road. This wintry view of Park Road looks towards Blackbrook, and shows Leyland trolleybus no. 101 returning to town, negotiating the railway bridge with its prominent 'Cephos' advertising. At Blackbrook, terminus of service 3A, there was a turning circle at the 'Ship Inn' and a loop in the inward wiring to allow trolleybuses from Haydock / Atherton to pass a 3A trolleybus waiting at the terminus. (N.N.Forbes)

Service No. 3   HAYDOCK (Rams Head)—ECCLESTON (Ackers Lane)
via Church Road, Clipsley Lane, West End Road, Blackbrook Road, Park Road, Higher Parr Street, Corporation Street, Cotham Street, Baldwin Street, Duke Street, Boundary Road, Knowsley Road, Mill Brow.

Service No. 3a   -   BLACKBROOK (Ship Inn)—ECCLESTON (Ackers Lane)
via Blackbrook Road, Park Road, Higher Parr Street, Corporation Street, Cotham Street, Baldwin Street, Duke Street, Boundary Road, Knowsley Road, Mill Brow.

Service No. 5   SEFTON PLACE—ECCLESTON (Ackers Lane)
via Baldwin Street, Duke Street, Boundary Road, Knowsley Road, Mill Brow.

MONDAYS TO SATURDAYS

42.   At Haydock, there was a reversing triangle at the 'Huntsman', also designated 3A, but this was not so regularly used as the turning point at Blackbrook. After passing the 'Huntsman', trolleybuses ran along Clipsley Lane and Church Road to reach the 'Ram's Head' terminus of service 3. This pre-war commercial postcard at Church Road shows the rear of one of St Helens' Ransomes six-wheelers, no. 114 proceeding on the Atherton service. (Authors collection)

43.   Nearing the end of a journey on service 3 to Haydock is 'Johannesburg' no. 165, seen here in Church Road. This type of vehicle was not usually seen on this route, or the long route to Atherton due to their higher powered motors which tended to drain the power from any SLT trolleybus in the same section. (J.C.Hillmer, Omnibus Society collection)

44.   The Haydock (Ram's Head) terminus of route 3 is seen here. One of the 1945 'utility' Sunbeams has reversed on the triangle, and is waiting to turn back onto Church Road and return to St Helens. South Lancashire Guy six-wheeler no. 11 is passing on the route to Atherton. This point was the boundary between St Helens and SLT owned wiring. (J.Copland / A.D.Packer)

45.   In the centre of Ashton in Makerfield, there was a reversing triangle at Princess Road. This was used to turn trolleybuses from both the St Helens and Atherton directions. Here, on 3rd November 1956, South Lancashire Guy 4-wheeler no 39 is reversing into Princess Road, whilst in the distance is St Helens 'utility' Sunbeam no. 313. St Helens vehicles terminating here showed service 2. SLT no. 39 is working to Haydock, and will follow the Corporation vehicle. (E.K.Stretch)

46. The almost universal type of vehicle operated by St Helens on the joint route to Atherton was the ten 'utility' Sunbeams dating from 1945. No. 307 crosses the railway at Hindley South Station, followed by a Lancashire United Guy motorbus.
(Online Transport Archive)

47. Much of the route was through drab industrial scenery, typified by this view of no. 309 at Dangerous Corner, between Hindley and Atherton.
(J.Batty / Online Transport Archive)

48. As mentioned earlier, it was very unusual to see other types of St Helens vehicle running on the Atherton route, other than the 'utility' Sunbeams. This scene is at Gibfield, and shows Leyland no. 102 leaving Atherton on a 'Private' working, most probably a driver familiarisation run.
(J.Batty / Online Transport Archive)

Joint Service   St. Helens Corporation Transport—South Lancashire Transport Company

ST. HELENS (Sefton Place)—HAYDOCK—ASHTON—PLATT BRIDGE—ATHERTON (Punch Bowl)

Service Nos. : 1 St. Helens—Atherton   2 St. Helens—Ashton   3 St. Helens—Haydock (Rams Head)

via Church Street, Higher Parr Street, Park Road, Blackbrook Road, West End Road, Clipsley Lane, Church Road, Penny Lane, Lodge Lane, Ashton, Bolton Road, Lily Lane, Platt Bridge, Liverpool Road, Hindley, Atherton Road, Wigan Road.

MONDAY TO SATURDAY

	S	S				S				Z								Z			Z
	AM	AM	AM	AM	AM	AM	AM	AM	AM	AM	AM	AM	AM	AM	AM	AM	AM	AM	AM	AM	AM
St. Helens (Sefton Place) ...dep	...	...	...	...	...	4 15	...	...	...	...	4 42	4 45	4 54	5 06	5 18	5 24	5 s30	5 36	5 42		
Haydock (Huntsman) .... "	...	...	...	...	...	4 30	...	...	...	...	4 57	5 00	5 09	5 21	5 33	5 39	5 45	5 51	5 57		
Haydock (Rams Head) .... "	...	...	...	...	...	4 38	...	...	...	...	5 04	...	5 16	5 28	5 40	5 46	5 55	6 00	6 07		
Ashton (Robin Hood) .... "	...	...	...	...	...	...	...	...	...	...	5*12	...	5*24	5*36	5*48	...	6 05	...	6 17		
Platt Bridge Depot .... "	4 35	4 47	4 50	4 59	5 02	...	5 11	5 14	5 23	5 26	5 35	...	5 47	5 59	6 11	...	6 23	...	6 35		
Hindley (Bird-in-Hand) ...... "	4 40	4 52	4 55	5 04	5 07	...	5 16	5 19	5 28	5 31	5 40	...	5 52	6 04	6 16	...	6 28	...	6 40		
Atherton (Punch Bowl) ......arr	4 57	5 09	...	5 21	...	...	5 33	...	5 45	...	5 57	...	6 09	6 21	6 33	...	6 45	...	6 57		

	AM	AM	AM	AM					PM	PM	PM	PM	PM	PM	PM	PM	PM	PM	PM	PM
St. Helens (Sefton Place) ...dep	5 54	6 00	6 06		and		and		8 30	8 36	8 42	8 48	8 54	9 00	9 06	9 12	9 18	9 24		
Haydock (Huntsman) .... "	6 09	6 14	6 21		every		every		8 45	8 50	8 57	9 02	9 09	9 14	9 21	9 26	9 33	9 38		
Haydock (Rams Head) .... "	6 19	6 22	6 31		12 mins.		6 mins.		8 55	8 58	9 07	9 10	9 19	9 22	9 31	9 34	9 43	9 46		
Ashton (Robin Hood) .... "	6 29	...	6 41		through		Sefton Place		9 05	...	9 17	...	9 28	...	9 41	...	9 52	...		
Platt Bridge Depot .... "	6 47	...	6 59		to		to		9 23	...	9 35	...	9 49	...	9 59	...	10 13			
Hindley (Bird-in-Hand) ...... "	6 52	...	7 04		Atherton		Rams Head		9 28	...	9 40	...	9 54	...	10 04	...	10 18			
Atherton (Punch Bowl) ......arr	7 09	...	7 21		until		until		9 45	...	9 57	...	10 12	...	10 21	...	10 36			

	PM	PM	PM	PM	PM	PM	PM	PM	PM	PM	PM	PM	PM	PM	PM	PM	PM	PM	PM	PM
St. Helens (Sefton Place) ...dep	9 30	9 36	9 42	9 48	9 54	1010	1006	1012	1018	1024	1030	1036	1042	1048	1054	1100	1106	1112	1120	
Haydock (Huntsman) .... "	9 45	9 50	9 57	1002	1009	1014	1021	1026	1033	1038	1045	1050	1057	1102	1109	1114	1121	1126	1135	
Haydock (Rams Head) .... "	9 55	9 58	1007	1010	1019	1022	1031	1034	1043	1046	1055	1058	1107	1110	1119	1122	1131	1134	1145	
Ashton (Robin Hood) .... "	1004	...	1016	...	1028	...	1041	...	1053	...	1105	...	1117	...	1129	...	1140	...	1154	
Platt Bridge Depot .... "	1025	...	1037	...	1049	...	1059	...	1111	...	1123	...	1135	...	1147	...				
Hindley (Bird-in-Hand) ...... "	1030	...	1042	...	1054	...	1104	...	...	...	...	...	...	...	...	...				
Atherton (Punch Bowl) ......arr	1048	...	1100	...	1112	...	...	...	...	...	...	...	...	...	...	...				

S—Saturdays only   Z—Not on Saturdays   *—Change Vehicles

For Service between Ackers Lane, Sefton Place, Rams Head, Service No. 3, see separate Timetables

49.   St Helens no. 307 has reached the terminal stop in Wigan Road Atherton and will shortly move forward to negotiate the reversing triangle, the frogs of which are just visible at the top of the photograph. Also visible is the wiring connection from Wigan Road into Mealhouse Lane on the right. This was used by SLT vehicles transferring from their Platt Bridge depot to the main depot at Howe Bridge, Atherton. (P.J.Taylor collection)

50.   The reversing movement at Atherton entailed placing the vehicle across Wigan Road, then reversing into Lambeth Street. The wires at the extremity of the reverser were suspended above the SLT trolleybus wiring turning into Mealhouse Lane. No. 112 is in position and about to reverse. In 1955 this vehicle was experimentally fitted with trolley retrievers, and evidently this view predates this event. (C.Carter)

51.   After completing the reversing movement, trolleybuses waited on the wrong side of Lambeth Street before returning to St Helens. This was in order to ease the tight turn left back into Wigan Road. No. 309 is seen in this position. (P.Caunt / Ribble Enthusiasts Club)

52.   On 19th June 1956, just a few months before the route was converted to motorbuses, St Helens post-war highbridge Sunbeam no. 380 was allocated to the Atherton route. Prior to 1953 this would have been impossible due to the low bridge near Hindley, which had been removed in that year. This was the only recorded occasion where a highbridge trolleybus (of either operator) ran on this service, and the reason for it is not known. The vehicle remained on the route all day, allowing Keith Stretch to photograph no. 380 in Lambeth Street. (E.K.Stretch)

PARR

53.   The Parr route branched off the Atherton wires in Higher Parr Street at Finger Post, running along Ashcroft Street. The terminus was at this turning circle within the carriageway at the junction of Derbyshire Hill Road and Fleet Lane. Ransomes trolleybus no. 106 is seen turning here when the route was opened in 1929. (G.Sandford collection)

54.   A post-war view of Sunbeam 'utility' no. 114 making the turn at Parr terminus. Route 4 was a through service to Moss Bank. A short working turning point along the Parr route was provided at Parr Library which was service 4A, or service 5A running through to Ackers Lane. This turning circle was replaced in 1952 by one at Boardman's Lane, to which the '4A' route number was applied. (J.Fozard)

ST HELENS JUNCTION

55.   This route served the railway station of this name which was on the pioneering Liverpool and Manchester Railway, two miles from St Helens centre. An interesting feature of this route was at the low bridges situated where Warrington New Road became Peasley Cross Lane. These required the use of lowbridge vehicles. When the post-war highbridge vehicles were put into service, the first of this type in the fleet, the General Manager Edgley Cox devised a warning device which activated a roof mounted power cut off switch if any of the new vehicles inadvertently approached the bridge. This was achieved by suspending the nearside trolley wire at the bridge approach at a lower level towards the pavement, thereby forcing the negative trolley boom down towards roof level and activating the power cut-off switch. This view of pre-war Leyland no. 129 demonstrates the arrangement, its negative boom being visible in the depressed position. In 1948, no. 129 had been one of the last pre-war vehicles to receive a replacement East Lancashire body and it was withdrawn from service in 1952, hardly value for money. (British Trolleybus Society collection)

Service No. 4   PARR (Platt Street)—BALDWIN STREET—MOSS BANK
via Derbyshire Hill Road, Broad Oak Road, Chancery Lane, Ashcroft Street, Higher Parr Street, Corporation Street, Baldwin Street, North Road, City Road, Moss Bank Road

MONDAY TO FRIDAY

	AM	AM	AM	AM	AM		AM	AM	AM	AM	AM	PM	AM	PM		PM
Parr (Platt Street) ....dep	...	4 55	...	5 11	...	5 27	and	11 19	...	11 30	11 35	11 42	...	11 51	12 00	and	5 48
Bulls Head .... ,,	...	5 02	...	5 18	...	5 34	every	11 26	...	11 37	11 42	11 49	...	11 58	12 07	every	5 55
Baldwin Street .... ,,	4 54	5 10	5 18	5 26	5 34	5 42	8 mins.	11 34	11 39	11 45	11 51	11 57	12 03	12 09	12 15	6 mins.	6 06
Moss Bank ....arr	5 02	5 18	5 26	5 34	5 42	5 50	until	11 42	11 48	11 54	12 00	12 06	12 12	12 18	12 24	until	6 14

	PM	PM	PM	PM	PM	PM	PM		PM	PM	PM	PM				
Parr (Platt Street) ....dep	5 54	6 00	6 06	6 15	6 18	6 23	6 31	and	11 03	11 11	11 19	11 33	...	...	...	...
Bulls Head .... ,,	6 01	6 07	6 13	6 22	6 25	6 30	6 38	every	11 10	11 18	11 26	11 40	...	...	...	...
Baldwin Street .... ,,	6 09	6 14	6 22	6 30	6 33	6 38	6 46	8 mins.	11 18	11 26	11 34	11 48	...	...	...	...
Moss Bank ....arr	...	6 22	6 30	6 38	...	6 46	6 54	until	11 26	...	...	...	...	...	...	...

SATURDAY

	AM	AM	AM	AM	AM	AM	AM		AM		AM	AM	AM	AM		AM
Parr (Platt Street) ....dep	...	4 55	...	5 11	...	5 27	5 35	5 43	and	11 19	...	11 30	11 35	11 42	...	11 51
Bulls Head .... ,,	...	5 02	...	5 18	...	5 34	5 42	5 50	every	11 26	...	11 37	11 42	11 49	...	11 58
Baldwin Street .... ,,	4 54	5 10	5 18	5 26	5 34	5 42	5 50	5 58	8 mins	11 34	11 39	11 45	11 51	11 57	12 03	12 09
Moss Bank ....arr	5 02	5 18	5 26	5 34	5 42	5 50	5 58	6 06	until	11 42	11 48	11 54	12 00	12 06	12 12	12 18

	PM		PM	PM	PM	PM	PM	PM	PM		PM	PM	PM	PM	PM	PM
Parr (Platt Street) ....dep	12 00	and	5 48	5 54	6 00	6 06	6 15	6 18	6 23	and	8 07	...	8 18	8 23	8 31	...	8 39
Bulls Head .... ,,	12 07	every	5 55	6 01	6 07	6 13	6 22	6 25	6 30	every	8 14	...	8 25	8 30	8 38	...	8 46
Baldwin Street .... ,,	12 15	6 mins	6 06	6 09	6 14	6 22	6 30	6 33	6 38	8 mins	8 22	8 27	8 33	8 39	8 45	8 51	8 57
Moss Bank ....arr.	12 24	until	6 14	...	6 22	6 30	6 38	...	6 46	until	8 30	8 36	8 42	8 48	8 54	9 00	9 06

	PM	PM	PM	PM	PM	PM	PM		PM	PM	PM	PM	PM	PM	PM	
Parr (Platt Street)..........dep	8 47	8 55	9 00	9 06	9 12	9 18	and	10 48	10 54	11 00	11 06	11 12	11 18	11 24	11 33	...	...
Bulls Head .... ,,	8 54	9 02	9 07	9 13	9 19	9 25	every	10 55	11 01	11 07	11 13	11 19	11 25	11 31	11 40	...	...
Baldwin Street .... ,,	9 03	9 09	9 15	9 21	9 27	9 33	6 mins	11 03	11 09	11 18	11 21	11 27	11 33	11 39	11 48	...	...
Moss Bank .... arr	9 12	9 18	9 24	9 30	9 36	9 42	until	11 12	11 18	11 26	...	...	...	...	...	...	...

SUNDAY

	AM	AM	AM		AM		AM		AM	AM		PM	PM	PM	PM	PM
Parr (Platt Street) ....dep	...	5 35	and	11 15	...	11 35	...	11 55	12 05	and	1 35	...	1 45	1 55	2 05	2 15
Bulls Head .... ,,	...	5 42	every	11 22	...	11 42	...	12 02	12 12	every	1 42	...	1 52	2 02	2 12	2 22
Baldwin Street .... ,,	5 20	5 40	5 50	20 mins.	11 30	11 40	11 50	12 00	12 10	12 20	10 mins.	1 50	1 58	2 06	2 14	2 22	2 30
Moss Bank ....arr	5 28	5 48	5 58	until	11 38	11 48	11 58	12 08	12 18	12 28	until	1 58	2 06	2 14	2 22	2 30	2 38

	PM			PM	PM	PM	PM	PM	PM	PM						
Parr (Platt Street)..........dep	2 23	and	10 47	10 55	11 03	11 11	11 19	11 33	...	...	...	...	...			
Bulls Head .... ,,	2 30	every	10 54	11 02	11 10	11 18	11 26	11 40	...	...	...	...	...			
Baldwin Street .... ,,	2 38	8 mins.	11 02	11 10	11 18	11 26	11 34	11 48	...	...	...	...	...			
Moss Bank ....arr	2 46	until	11 10	11 18	11 26	...	...	...	...	...	...	...	...			

56.   Another view of the wiring arrangement on Warrington New Road, approaching the low bridges. (British Trolleybus Society collection)

57.   The terminus at St Helens Junction was in the form of a clockwise loop.
Here, on the last day of trolleybus operation on the route, one of the 1945 Sunbeam 'utility' vehicles turns from Junction Road into Station Road, where the terminal stop was located. Trolleybuses on this service, no. 6, ran through to Denton's Green. (N.N.Forbes)

58. The last trolleybus route to open was the service to Ackers Lane, this occurring in 1943. It branched off the Denton's Green route at Duke Street, and ran along Boundary Road and Knowsley Road. In Boundary Road, alongside Queens Park, Leyland no. 131 carefully negotiates a flood en route to the terminus. (G. Sandford collection)

Service No. 6

DENTONS GREEN—BALDWIN STREET—ST. HELENS JUNCTION

via Dentons Green Lane, Duke Street, Baldwin Street, Church Street, Warrington New Road, Peasley Cross Lane, Robins Lane, Station Road

MONDAY TO FRIDAY

		*		*	*	*	*	*			and					and	
	AM	AM	AM	AM	AM	AM	AM	AM	AM	AM	every	AM	AM	AM		every	AM
Dentons Green ....dep	...	5 02	...	5 20	...	...	...	...	6 08	6 16	8 mins	7 12	7 18	7 24		6 mins	8 48
Baldwin Street .... ,,	4 40	5 10	5 20	5 28	5 44	5 52	6 00	6 08	6 16	6 24	until	7 20	7 26	7 32		until	8 56
St. Helens Hospital .... ,,	4 48	5 20	5 28	5 36	5 52	6 00	6 08	6 16	6 24	6 32		7 28	7 34	7 40			9 04
St. Helens Junction ....arr	4 56	5 28	5 36	5 44	6 00	6 08	6 16	6 24	6 32	6 40		7 36	7 42	7 48			9 12

	AM		AM		PM	PM	PM	PM		and	PM	PM	PM	PM			
Dentons Green ....dep	8 56	and	1136	and	6 00	6 08	6 12	6 16		every	1056	1104	1112	1124	...	...	...
Baldwin Street .... ,,	9 04	every	1144	every	6 08	6 16	6 20	6 24		8 mins	1104	1118	1120	1132	...	...	...
St. Helens Hospital .... ,,	9 12	8 mins	1152	6 mins	6 16	6 24	...	6 32		until	1112	1126	...	...	...	...	...
St. Helens Junction ....arr	9 20	until	1200	until	6 24	6 32	...	6 40			1120	1133	...	...	...	...	...

SATURDAY

	*		*		*	*	*	*		and		and		and		
	AM	AM	AM	AM	AM	AM	AM	AM		every	AM	every	AM	every	AM	
Dentons Green ....dep	...	5 02	...	5 20	...	...	...	6 08		8 mins	7 12	6 mins	8 48	8 mins	1136	
Baldwin Street .... ,,	4 40	5 10	5 20	5 28	5 44	5 52	6 00	6 08	6 16	until	7 20	until	8 56	until	1144	
St. Helens Hospital .... ,,	4 48	5 18	5 28	5 36	5 52	6 00	6 08	6 16	6 24		7 28		9 04		1152	
St. Helens Junction ....arr	4 56	5 28	5 36	5 44	6 00	6 08	6 16	6 24	6 32		7 36		9 12		1200	

	AM		PM	PM	PM		and	PM	PM		and	PM	PM	PM	PM
Dentons Green ....dep	1142	and	2 06	2 08	2 13		every	6 08	6 14		and	1108	1114	1120	1126
Baldwin Street .... ,,	1150	every	2 14	2 16	2 21		5 mins	6 16	6 22		every	1118	1122	1128	1134
St. Helens Hospital .... ,,	1158	6 mins	2 22	2 24	2 29		until	6 24	6 30		6 mins	1126	...	...	...
St. Helens Junction ....arr	1206	until	2 30	2 32	2 37			6 32	6 38		until	1134	...	...	...

* Indicates—Starts from Ormskirk Street

59.   The Ackers Lane terminus was at the junction of Mill Brow and Ackers Lane. Leyland no. 123, with 1945 built East Lancashire body, stands at the terminus before returning to the town centre on service 5. Also serving this point were service 3 through to Haydock and service 5A through to Parr Library. There was one short working turning point along the route, this being at the junction of Knowsley Road and Dunriding Lane, where a turning circle was provided for extra journeys run for home matches of the St Helens Rugby League Club.
(H.Luff / Online Transport Archive)

DENTON'S GREEN

60.   The Denton's Green route ran along Duke Street and Denton's Green Road, terminating at the junction of Rainford Road and Hard Lane. 1935 built Leyland no. 127, with Massey body is seen when new negotiating the turning circle. Note the passenger waiting shelter on the left. (R.Marshall collection)

61.   This view is of the Denton's Green terminus shortly before the route was abandoned in 1952. Leyland no. 132, from the same batch of vehicle shown in the previous view, but with 1945 built East Lancashire body, is seen turning round to return to St Helens Junction on service 6. (N.N.Forbes)

MOSS BANK

62.   The Moss Bank route ran north from the town centre via North Road and Windle. Between the latter point and the terminus, it crossed the East Lancashire Road on the level. In this view, 1945 Sunbeam 'utility' no. 106, en route to Moss Bank is waiting to cross this major highway. It opened to traffic in 1934 and was a direct road between Manchester and Liverpool. (N.N.Forbes)

63.   Moss Bank terminus was adjacent to the railway station at this point, which was on the direct railway line between St Helens and Ormskirk. It closed to passengers in June 1951. One of the final batch of Ransomes trolleybuses, no. 146, is seen at the terminal point. These 12 vehicles were the only pre-war vehicles to have two windows at the upper deck front. Note also the low-mounted headlights. (R.Marshall collection)

PRESCOT VIA RAINHILL

64.   After negotiating the town centre one way loop, trolleybuses outbound to Prescot joined the inbound wires at Croppers Hill. Here, Sunbeam no. 380 turns out of Liverpool Road on a service 8 journey to Prescot. In the left background is Westfield Street, where an LUT motorbus can be seen. (N.N.Forbes)

65.   At the 'Eccleston Arms' stop on Prescot Road is Sunbeam no. 376 on its way into the town centre. The 'Eccleston Arms' is out of view on the right. (P.Mitchell)

66.   At Toll Bar, (the junction of Prescot Road and Lugsmore Lane), the two routes to Prescot parted company, the clockwise service 7 turning into Lugsmore Lane. There was a turning circle here just west of the junction. In this view, BUT no 389, on service 8 is about to pass under the turning circle facing frog. Lugsmore Lane (service 7) goes off to the right in the background. (J.S.King)

67.   At Thatto Heath station (on the direct Liverpool – St Helens Shaw Street line), the trolleybuses crossed a bridge over the railway. BUT no. 388 has just negotiated the bridge, passing the 'Springfield Hotel', on a service 9 journey back to St Helens. These journeys turned round at Prescot and did not cover the full circle. (P.Mitchell)

68.   The bridge at Thatto Heath station was very narrow and arched, as is evident in this view of BUT no. 388 proceeding on service 9 towards Prescot where it will terminate and return to St Helens via Rainhill. (D.F.Parker)

FARE **3/4** | A **9600**

St. Helens Corporation Transport
WORKMAN'S PREPAID TICKET

VALID FOR ONE INWARD AND ONE OUTWARD
JOURNEY ON EACH OF 5 CONSECUTIVE DAYS
OVER A 8D. WORKPEOPLE'S RETURN FARE
STAGE.

Route   Between Stages

No.   &

OUT	MR.	IN
---	MRS.	---
Mon	MISS	**Mon**
Tues	ADDRESS	**Tues**
Wed		**Wed**
Thurs	WEEK COMMENCING	**Thurs**
FRI or SUN	DATE SUNDAY MONDAY	FRI or SUN

FOR CONDITIONS — SEE BACK.
NOT TRANSFERABLE

Service No. 7
ST. HELENS (Bridge Street)—RAINHILL—PRESCOT—PORTICO—ST. HELENS (Sefton Place)
via Liverpool Road, Prescot Road, Lugsmore Lane, Thatto Heath Road, Nutgrove Road, Rainhill Road, St. Helens Road, New Road, Warrington Road, Prescot, St. Helens Road, Prescot Road, Croppers Hill, Westfield Street

MONDAY TO FRIDAY

	AM	AM	AM	AM			AM			PM			PM			PM	PM	
St. Helens (Bridge Street) ......dep	4 45	...	4 50	5 04	and		6 57	and		8 57	and		12 27	and		5 21	and	11 06	11 18	...
Toll Bar	4 54	...	4 57	5 11			7 04			9 04			12 34			5 28		11 13	11 25	...
Mental Hospital	5 00	...	5 03	5 17			7 10			9 10			12 40			5 34		11 19	11 31	...
Rainhill Bridge	...	...	5 08	5 22	every		7 15	every		9 15	every		12 45	every		5 39	every	11 24	11 36	...
Prescot (Cable Works)	...	...	5 14	5 28			7 21			9 21			12 51			5 45		11 30	11 42	...
Prescot (Hare and Hounds)	...	...	5 17	5 31	7½		7 24	6		9 24	7½		12 54	6		5 48	7½	11 33	11 45	...
Eccleston Park	...	...	5 21	5 35			7 28			9 28			12 58			5 52		11 37	11 49	...
Portico	...	5 00	5 22	5 36	mins.		7 29	mins.		9 29	mins.		12 59	mins.		5 53	mins.	11 38	11 50	...
Toll Bar	...	5 05	5 26	5 40			7 33			9 33			1 03			5 57		11 42	11 54	...
St. Helens (Sefton Place)........arr	...	5 14	5 34	5 48	until		7 41	until		9 41	until		1 11	until		6 05	until	11 50	12 02	...

SATURDAY

	AM	AM	AM	AM	AM	AM			AM			AM			PM			PM	PM	
St. Helens (Bridge Street) ......dep	4 45	...	4 50	5 04	5 12	5 19	and		6 57	and		8 57	and		12 27	and		11 09	11 27	...
Toll Bar	4 54	...	4 57	5 11	5 19	5 26			7 04			9 04			12 34			11 16	11 25	...
Mental Hospital	5 00	...	5 03	5 17	5 25	5 32			7 10			9 10			12 40			11 22	11 31	...
Rainhill Bridge	...	...	5 08	5 22	5 30	5 37	every		7 15	every		9 15	every		12 45	every		11 27	11 36	...
Prescot (Cable Works)	...	...	5 14	5 28	5 36	5 43			7 21			9 21			12 51			11 33	11 42	...
Prescot (Hare and Hounds)	...	...	5 17	5 31	5 39	5 46	7½		7 24	6		9 24	7½		12 54	6		11 36	11 45	...
Eccleston Park	...	...	5 21	5 35	5 43	5 50			7 28			9 28			12 58			11 40	11 49	...
Portico	...	5 00	5 22	5 36	5 44	5 51	mins.		7 29	mins.		9 29	mins.		12 59	mins.		11 41	11 50	...
Toll Bar	...	5 05	5 26	5 40	5 48	5 55			7 33			9 33			1 03			11 45	11 54	...
St. Helens (Sefton Place)........arr	...	5 14	5 34	5 48	5 56	6 03	until		7 41	until		9 41	until		1 11	until		11 53	12 02	...

SUNDAY

	AM	AM			PM	PM			PM			PM			PM			PM			
St. Helens (Bridge Street) ...... dep	5 25	6 08	and		12 23	12 32	and		1 55	and		5 01	and		6 54	and		11 18	...	...	...
Toll Bar	5 34	6 15			12 30	12 39			2 02			5 08			7 01			11 25	...	...	...
Mental Hospital	5 40	6 21			12 36	12 45			2 08			5 14			7 07			11 31	...	...	...
Rainhill Bridge	...	6 26	every		12 41	12 50	every		2 13	every		5 19	every		7 12	every		11 36	...	...	...
Prescot (Cable Works)	...	6 32			12 47	12 56			2 19			5 25			7 18			11 42	...	...	...
Prescot (Hare and Hounds)	...	6 35	15		12 50	12 59	7½		2 22	6		5 28	7½		7 21	6		11 45	...	...	...
Eccleston Park	...	6 39			12 54	1 03			2 26			5 32			7 25			11 49	...	...	...
Portico	...	6 40	mins.		12 55	1 04	mins.		2 27	mins.		5 33	mins.		7 26	mins.		11 50	...	...	...
Toll Bar	...	6 44			12 59	1 08			2 31			5 37			7 30			11 54	...	...	...
St. Helens (Sefton Place) ...... arr	...	6 52	until		1 07	1 16	until		2 39	until		5 45	until		7 38	until		12 02	...	...	...

69.   At Nutgrove (the junction of Nutgrove Road and Rainhill Road) was the Rainhill Hospital Gates. As can be seen, there was a full circle of wiring here. At hospital visiting times, extra journeys ran to this point, and two of these are evident here. On the left (facing St Helens) is Sunbeam no. 375, and on the right is sister vehicle no. 376. Compare this view with photograph no 2. (J.S.King)

70.   BUT no. 383 pauses at Nutgrove working on a service 8 journey back to St Helens. Note the conductress with TIM ticket machine standing behind the vehicle. The Rainhill Hospital Gates are visible in the background. (D.F.Parker)

71.   Proceeding from Nutgrove towards Prescot along Rainhill Road, the route passed between the high walls of the hospital. This late 1920s view shows Ransomes no. 100 in this section working on the Rainhill to Prescot shuttle service. (R.Marshall collection)

72.   In Rainhill Road, the first of the post-war vehicles, Sunbeam no. 374, proceeds towards Prescot with the hospital wall on the right. (P.Mitchell)

73.   At the southern end of Rainhill Road, Sunbeam no. 377 is seen outside the Co-operative store. In the distance the route curves to the right into New Road. (P.Mitchell)

74.   One of the original 1927 Garretts, no. 103 (formerly no. 3) is seen pausing at the 'Coach and Horses' public house at Rainhill. (G.Sandford collection)

75.   This is the same location as the previous photograph, but taken some thirty years later. Sunbeam no. 378 comes round the curve from Rainhill Road into New Road passing the 'Coach and Horses'. (J.S.King)

76.   Passengers board BUT no. 383 in New Road near Rainhill station. The 'Coach and Horses' is in the far distance on the right. This rear view shows the arrangement of the upper deck emergency door on these vehicles, which incorporated a platform for overhead linesmen to access the roof. (J.S.King)

77.   At the southern end of New Road, trolleybuses turned right onto the busy Warrington Road (A57). This was very near to Rainhill Station, and the hump in the road beyond the front of the vehicle is the arch over the line. This was built at a 34 degree skew across the line, and the 'skew arch' was hailed as an engineering triumph when it was built in the 1820s. (J.C.Gillham)

78.   The run along the A57 to → 79.   Nearing Prescot was the large area of the Cable
Prescot was about two miles in Works, latterly known at the British Insulated Callender's Cables
length. About half-way along this Co (BICC), suppliers, amongst other products, of trolleybus
stretch, Sunbeam no. 381 is seen overhead line equipment. The main offices had their frontage on
heading for Rainhill and St Helens. the west side of the A57. Seen passing the offices in about 1930
It has just passed Longview Road. is Garrett no. 101 (formerly no. 1), as it nears Prescot. Note the
(P.Mitchell) setted road surface. (G.Sandford collection)

→   80. Outside the BICC offices, is Sunbeam no. 378 en route to Prescot and St Helens. There
was a short working turning circle here, allowing trolleybuses to turn from the Rainhill direction.
The facing frog of this can be seen in the upper left of this view. Note that no. 378 only carries half
a fleetname, a consequence of panel repairs. (P.Mitchell)

PRESCOT

81.   The main stop in Prescot for trolleybuses returning to St Helens via Rainhill was outside the, Reform Club in Warrington Road. This late 1940s view pre-dates the arrival of the post war vehicles, and shows a much battered Ransomes no. 151 waiting here before departure. (W.J.Haynes)

ZX 0259		
1/18	2d	34/17
2/19		33/16
3/20		32/15
4/21		31/14
5/22		30/13
6/23		29/12
7/24		28/11
8/25		27/10
9/26		CHILD

ST. HELENS CORP'N TRANSPORT.
This ticket is available from the stage at which it is punched-and must be shewn or given up on demand.   A.T.Ltd.
NOT TRANSFERABLE.

82.   Outside the Reform Club at Prescot is Sunbeam no. 177, in fairly new condition. Note the licence number and seating capacity lettering over the windscreens, a feature later dispensed with. This vehicle was renumbered to 377 in mid-1955. In the left background is Wycherley Street, which formed part of the Prescot turning facility. (P.Mitchell)

83.   The main stop for trolleybuses arriving from Rainhill, and returning to St Helens via Portico was across the road from the Reform Club outside the 'Hare and Hounds' public house. BUT no. 385 is seen here, with Sunbeam no. 375 at the opposite stop on 1st March 1958. (R.Brook)

84. This pleasant animated scene shows BUT no. 387 waiting outside the 'Hare and Hounds'. (C.W.Routh)

→ 85. This early 1950s scene at Prescot shows BUT no. 185, and behind this is one of St Helens' RT type motorbuses operating on service 97 from Prescot to Peasely Cross Lane. Unlike no. 185, these vehicles, despite being of highbridge construction, were just low enough to pass under the low bridges at the latter point. (R.Marshall/The Omnibus Society)

→ 86. Sunbeam no. 378 has just left the 'Hare and Hounds' terminus (visible in the left background), and is approaching the traffic lights at the junction with St Helens Road. Although it is now heading for St Helens via the direct route, it is still showing (incorrectly) 'Rainhill'. (J.C.Gillham)

87.	At almost the same spot as the previous photograph, BUT no. 384 is on a service 9 journey terminating at Prescot, and will proceed via the turning loop to return to St Helens via Rainhill. In the right background can be seen the trailing frog which allowed vehicles to turn from the Portico direction, by using the Warrington Road / Wycherley Street junction as a reversing triangle. (J.S.King)

↓ 89. - 90.	This is the 'King's Arms' junction of Warrington Road (to the right) and St Helens Road (receding into the left distance). These separate images, put together, form a panorama of this junction. Sunbeam no. 380 is about to turn into Warrington Road to reach the Reform Club terminus. On the right, BUT no. 382 is seen turning into St Helens Road whilst a police constable keeps an eye on the photographer. Just visible in the left background of photograph no. 89 is the facing frog leading into Grosvenor Road. (R.Brook)

88.   When the Prescot trolleybus route was made into a circular service in 1936, the original turning circle in Warrington Road was replaced by a reversing triangle in Wycherley Street, This allowed turns from either direction. During the war, in 1942, a safer arrangement was provided, this being a 'round the houses' loop via Grosvenor Road and Wycherley Street. The new arrangement retained a reversing facility for vehicles turning from the Portico direction, because the left hand turn from St Helens Road into Grosvenor Road was too tight for trolleybuses to use. This view shows Sunbeam no. 378 in Wycherley Street, about to turn left into Warrington Road at the Reform Club on a terminating service 9 working. Note that the conductor is pulling the frog handle, the frog being normally set for the reversing movement. (D.F.Parker)

91. A scene at the same junction, but some nine years earlier. After the replacement of the trams on the direct route to Prescot in 1936, the terminus of the Liverpool tram service, which had previously been in Warrington Road (see photograph no. 1), moved to a siding in St Helens Road, this track still being owned by St Helens Corporation. This arrangement lasted until June 1949, when the Liverpool trams on this route were converted to motorbuses. This view, taken just before the trams finished, shows Ransomes trolleybus no. 153. on service 7 passing a Liverpool tram. The special tram/trolleybus crossing in the wiring can be seen, which isolated the tram wire and trolleybus wires, allowing the tram to power through the crossing. The rather unkept trolleybus is showing route no. 7 in the aperture which before 1943 showed a destination. Note also that the sliding window at the rear upper deck is open. (N.N.Forbes)

PRESCOT VIA PORTICO

92.   In St Helens Road, heading for Prescot, is BUT no. 388. It is approaching the junction with Burrows Lane at Eccleston Lane Ends. (P.Mitchell)

93. At Portico Lane, there was a short working reversing triangle at the 'Grapes' public house. BUT no. 385 is passing this on a service 8 journey to Prescot. (P.Mitchell)

← 94. BUT no. 387 is seen approaching Portico Lane from the St Helens direction, with the exit wires of the reverser in view. This stretch of route was quite rural, as can be seen. Note the posse of cycling schoolboys. (N.N.Forbes)

95. Having just crossed the St Helens borough boundary, BUT no. 383 speeds towards Portico and Prescot on 28th June 1958, the last Saturday of trolleybus operation. Note the bracket arms on this section. (J.S.King)

Service No. 8

ST. HELENS (Bridge Street)—PORTICO—PRESCOT—RAINHILL—ST. HELENS (Sefton Place)

Via Liverpool Road, Prescot Road, St. Helens Road, Prescot, Warrington Road, New Road, St. Helens Road, Rainhill Road, Nutgrove Road, Thatto Heath Road, Lugsmore Lane, Prescot Road, Croppers Hill, Westfield Street.

MONDAY TO FRIDAY

	AM	AM	AM	AM		AM		AM		PM		PM		PM	PM
St. Helens (Bridge St.) ...dep	...	4 40	4 45	4 52		7 00		9 00		1230		5 12		11 09	11 18
Toll Bar ,,	...	4 47	4 54	4 59	and	7 07	and	9 07	and	1237	and	5 19	and	11 16	11 25
Portico ,,	...	4 51	5 00	5 03		7 11		9 11		1241		5 23		11 20	11 29
Eccleston Park ,,	...	4 52	...	5 04	every	7 12	every	9 12	every	1242	every	5 24	every	11 21	11 30
Prescot (Reform Club) ,,	...	4 56	...	5 08		7 16		9 16		1246		5 28		11 25	11 34
Prescot (Cable Works) ,,	...	4 59	...	5 11	7½	7 19	6	9 19	7½	1249	6	5 31	7½	11 28	11 37
Rainhill Bridge ,,	...	5 04	...	5 16		7 24		9 24		1254		5 36		11 33	11 42
Mental Hospital ,,	5 00	5 09	...	5 21	mins.	7 29	mins.	9 29	mins.	1259	mins.	5 41	mins.	11 38	11 47
Toll Bar ,,	5 05	5 15	...	5 27		7 35		9 35		1 05		5 47		11 44	11 53
St. Helens (Sefton Place) arr	5 14	5 24	...	5 36	until	7 44	until	9 44	until	1 14	until	5 56	until	11 53	1202

SATURDAY

	AM	AM	AM	AM	AM	AM	AM	AM		AM		AM		PM	PM
St. Helens (Bridge St.) ...dep	4 30	4 45	...	4 52	5 00	5 07	5 15	5 22		7 00		9 00		1230	11 18
Toll Bar ,,	4 37	4 54	...	4 59	5 07	5 14	5 22	5 29	and	7 07	and	9 07	and	1237	11 25
Portico ,,	4 41	5 00	...	5 03	5 11	5 18	5 26	5 33		7 11		9 11		1241	11 29
Eccleston Park ,,	4 42	...	...	5 04	5 12	5 19	5 27	5 34	every	7 12	every	9 12	every	1242	11 30
Prescot (Reform Club) ,,	4 46	...	...	5 08	5 16	5 23	5 31	5 38		7 16		9 16		1246	11 34
Prescot (Cable Works) ,,	4 49	...	...	5 11	5 19	5 26	5 34	5 41	7½	7 19	6	9 19	7½	1249	11 37
Rainhill Bridge ,,	4 54	...	...	5 16	5 24	5 31	5 39	5 46		7 24		9 24		1254	11 42
Mental Hospital ,,	4 59	...	5 00	5 21	5 29	5 36	5 44	5 51	mins.	7 29	mins.	9 29	mins.	1259	11 47
Toll Bar ,,	5 05	...	5 05	5 27	5 35	5 42	5 50	5 57		7 35		9 35		1 05	11 53
St. Helens (Sefton Place) arr	5 14	...	5 14	5 36	5 44	5 51	5 59	6 06	until	7 44	until	9 44	until	1 14	1202

SUNDAY

	AM	AM	AM		PM		PM		PM		PM		PM	PM
St. Helens (Bridge St.) ...dep	5 45	6 00	6 30		1230		1 52		4 58		6 57		11 09	11 18	...
Toll Bar ,,	5 52	6 07	6 37	and	1237	and	1 59	and	5 05	and	7 04	and	11 16	11 25	...
Portico ,,	5 56	6 11	6 41		1241		2 03		5 09		7 08		11 20	11 29	...
Eccleston Park ,,	5 57	6 12	6 42	every	1242	every	2 04	every	5 10	every	7 09	every	11 21	11 30	...
Prescot (Reform Club) ,,	6 04	6 19	6 49	15	1249	7½	2 11	6	5 17	7½	7 16	6	11 25	11 34	...
Prescot (Cable Works) ,,	6 09	6 24	6 54		1254		2 16		5 22		7 21		11 28	11 37	...
Rainhill Bridge ,,	6 14	6 29	6 59	mins.	1259	mins.	2 21	mins.	5 27	mins.	7 26	mins.	11 33	11 42	...
Mental Hospital ,,	6 20	6 35	7 05		1 05		2 27		5 33		7 32		11 44	11 53	...
St. Helens (Sefton Place) arr	6 29	6 44	7 14	until	1 14	until	2 36	until	5 42	until	7 41	until	11 53	1202	...

96.	On the same day as the previous photograph, BUT no. 387 negotiates the curve at Eccleston Park, en route for Prescot. (J.S.King)

97.	At the Borough Boundary, St Helens Road becomes Prescot Road. Having diverged from service 7 at Toll Bar, Sunbeam no. 381 on service 8 is seen at the 'Grange Park Hotel', which has since been demolished. (P.Mitchell)

THE VEHICLES

98.   **1927   1 – 4   Garrett 'O' 4-wheel single deck
Registration numbers:
DJ 3243 - 3246**

These trolleybuses comprised the original fleet that replaced trams between Rainhill and Prescot. The Ransomes centre entrance bodies seated 35 passengers. They were renumbered 101 – 104 in 1929. From the end of 1936 they spent some time in store, but no. 2 was used as an illuminated vehicle in various guises (see photograph 112). The rest were renumbered again in October 1937, becoming 161, 163 and 164, when they returned to service. Final withdrawal came in July 1938. (G.Sandford collection)

ST HELENS CORPORATION LOW BRIDGE TROLLEYBUS

Chassis: Sunbeam MF2 built 1942.
Body: 8 foot wide by Massey.
Type: "Johannesburg" No. 157- 166.

Scale: 4 mm = 1 Foot.

DRAWING No.TB81

SCALE FEET: 0 1 2 3 4 5 6 7 8 9 10 11 12

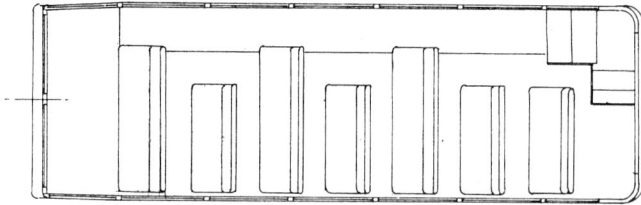

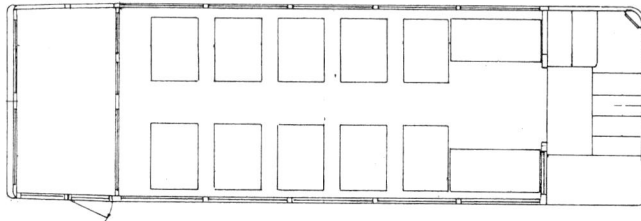

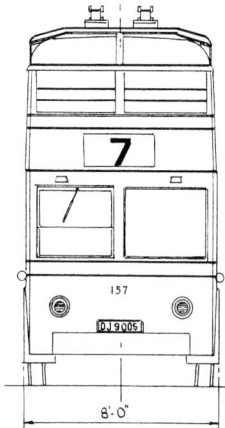

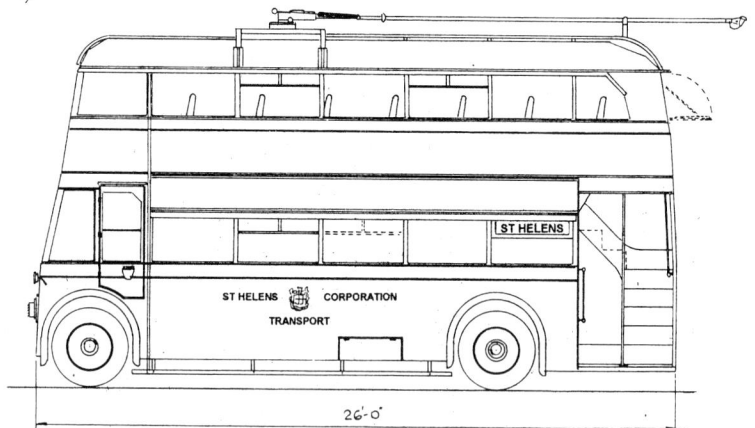

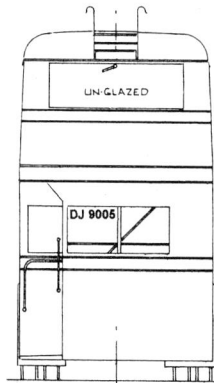

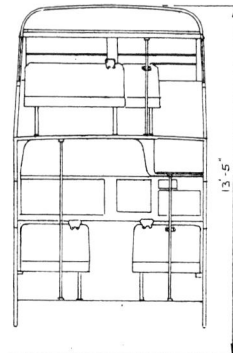

7

157

DJ 9005

ST HELENS

ST HELENS   CORPORATION
TRANSPORT

8'-0"

26'-0"

UN-GLAZED

DJ 9005

13'-5"

I have created this drawing using the standard "Austerity" 7'-6" wide bus as a basis and contrived the 8'-0" wide, low bridge upper deck from photographs and overall height.   Terry Russell February 2013.

DRAWN BY: TERRY RUSSELL. 23, THORNDEN, COWFOLD, HORSHAM. WEST SUSSEX. RH13 8AG
FOR THE FULL LIST OF OVER 1000 DRAWINGS AND MODEL TRAM PARTS VISIT MY WEB SITE
www.terryruselltrams.co.uk OR SEND 6 FIRST CLASS STAMPS FOR A PAPER COPY.

99.   **1928-29   5, 105 – 109**   **Ransomes 4-wheel single deck**
Registration numbers: DJ 3840, DJ 4081-4, ET 5968

The original fleet was augmented in 1928 by the arrival of a Ransomes single decker with Ransomes centre entrance body. This was renumbered from 5 to 100 in 1929, when a further five Ransomes were delivered for the Parr route. No. 109 bore a Rotherham registration number because it had been demonstrated there before delivery to St Helens. The first vehicle was renumbered again to 110 in 1934. This vehicle, with 105-7 was withdrawn in the summer of 1938, and the remaining two lasted until the outbreak of war. The photograph shows one of the 105-109 series in the 1930s style of livery. (G.Sandford collection)

100.   **1930**   **110 – 114**   **Ransomes 'D6' six-wheel double deck**
Registration numbers: DJ 4845 – 4849

These were the first double deckers in the fleet and were bought for operation on the joint service to Atherton. They had Ransomes lowbridge 60 seat bodies and two 40 hp motors of EMB manufacture. No. 110 was renumbered to 115 in 1934. They were all withdrawn in 1942. (R.Marshall collection)

101.　　1934 – 1937　　　116-120, 137-144
　　　　　　　　　　　　Ransomes D4 four-wheel double deck
　　　　　　　　　　　　Registration numbers:
　　　　　　　　　　　　　116-120 DJ 6051 - 6055　　　　　　　(1934)
　　　　　　　　　　　　　137-144 DJ 6863 – 6867, 7236 – 7238　(1937)

To replace the tram fleet, St Helens bought trolleybus chassis from both Ransomes and Leyland. Both types were bodied by Brush or Massey to a standard lowbridge 50 seat design, which incorporated a distinctive three window arrangement to the upper deck front. The Ransomes vehicles, detailed above were bodied by Brush (1934 batch) and Massey (1937 batch).

After the war, many of the 1937 batch had their bodywork rebuilt, but this did not affect their overall appearance. No 119. was rebodied by East Lancashire in 1943, the only Ransomes chassis to be so treated. All of the 1934 batch, except 119 were withdrawn in 1945, and the later batch was withdrawn between late 1949 and early 1952. No. 119 lasted until the end of 1950. The photograph shows no. 120 when new at Sefton Place. The route boards were a short lived facility. Note the painted 'via' between the two destination apertures. (Author's collection)

102.   As stated in the previous caption, the rebuilding of vehicles after the war did not generally affect their appearance. One exception was Ransomes no. 139 which was rebuilt with a two window upper deck front, producing a rather unattractive clash of styling. It is seen here in Baldwin Street in the new livery. It was withdrawn in January 1952. (P.J.Taylor collection)

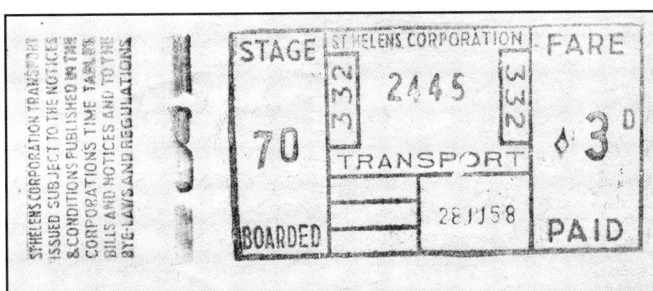

103. **1934 – 1937   121-136, 101-104**
Leyland TBD2 four-wheel double deck
Registration numbers:

121-125 DJ 6106, 6120 – 6123	**(1934)**
126-136 DJ 6453 – 6463,	**(1935)**
101-104 DJ 7428 – 7431	**(1937)**

Three batches of Leyland four-wheelers were purchased in the 1930s, the first batch having Brush bodies, and the remainder Massey bodies. All were rebodied by East Lancashire between 1944 and 1948 (see photographs 107 and 108). By 1952 all had been withdrawn except the 1937 batch which ran until late 1956, when the Haydock route closed. By this time they had been renumbered to 301-4, the only pre-war vehicles to be so treated. The photograph shows Brush bodied no. 124 before delivery to St Helens. The extra long trolley booms are said to have been provided so that these vehicles could reach the kerb when operating under South Lancashire wiring. Note that there was no provision on the pre-war trolleybuses for an emergency exit at the rear end of the upper deck, although there was a sliding pane which was used by staff to gain access to the trolley gear on the roof. (Author's collection)

➔ **104.   1938   145-156**
Ransomes D4 four-wheel
double deck
Registration numbers:
DJ 8120-8131

The final batch of pre-war trolleybuses comprised twelve Ransomes chassis with Massey bodies to an improved design with only two windows at the front upper deck. They also received a new livery style which was not perpetuated. Most were rebuilt after the war, and all were withdrawn by early 1952. No. 150 is shown here, posed in Denton's Green Road when new. The revised livery style is evident. (J.S.King collection)

105.   1942   157-166
Sunbeam MF2 four-wheel
double deck
Registration numbers:
DJ 9006-9015

Ten Sunbeam MF2 chassis, with Massey lowbridge 50 seat 'utility' bodies were allocated to St Helens by the Ministry of War Transport in 1942. The chassis had been part of an order for 25 built for Johannesburg. Wartime conditions meant that they could not be exported and they were distributed to home trolleybus systems. Bradford received ten and Nottingham the remaining five chassis. Because they were 8 feet wide, and therefore illegal for use in Britain, special dispensation had to be agreed with the Ministry for their use. They were delivered in wartime grey livery, and were initially used on the Prescot services. Their higher powered motors precluded their use on the Atherton route following objections from SLT - their vehicles were reduced to a crawl when a 'Johannesburg' vehicle was in the same section. The photograph shows no. 158 undergoing the tilt test before delivery. Note the drab overall grey livery and the large destination box, which initially showed a route number only. (G.Sandford collection)

106. All the 'Johannesburg' vehicles were rebuilt by various agencies after the war, resulting in a revised destination indicator layout, and they ran until the end of 1955 when the Parr route was closed, by which time they had been renumbered 357 – 366. No. 158, which had been rebuilt by Air Despatch of Cardiff in 1948, is seen at Bridge Street in the mainly red livery. Note the nearside cab door – the only access to the cab for the driver, and the 'half crest' on the dash panel. (R.Marshall)

➜ 107. **1944 – 1948   121-136, 101-104**
Rebodied Leyland TBD2
Between 1944 and 1948, all the pre-war Leyland trolleybuses, numbering 20 vehicles, were rebuilt with new East Lancashire bodies following the similar treatment of Ransomes no. 119 in 1943. All except nos. 101 – 104 were withdrawn by early 1952, resulting in some of these vehicles having very short lives in their new state. Nos. 101 to 104 were withdrawn in 1956 after the closure of the Haydock route (on which they were regular performers), by which time they had been renumbered to 301 – 304. There were two frontal styles of body. Nos. 132 and 136, rebodied in 1945 and seen here after withdrawal, have the more angular style, looking very much like the 1945 'utility' Roe bodies. (P.Mitchell)

108.   The other, more stylish looking type of East Lancashire body is seen in the official view of no. 135 (also rebodied in 1945) at Sefton Place before re-entering service. (Omnibus Society collection)

109. 1945 105-114 Sunbeam W four-wheel double deck
Registration numbers: DJ 9183-9192

Ten Sunbeam 'W' vehicles, with Roe 'utility' lowbridge bodies, entered service just after the hostilities had ceased in 1945. These were the first trolleybuses in the fleet to have off-side cab doors. They were also 'go –anywhere' vehicles, being seen on all the routes, especially the Atherton service. All survived to be renumbered to 305 – 314 in 1955, and all but two were withdrawn after the Atherton route closure. The survivors were nos. 311 and 312, which were then used for training and occasional service use. The last survivor was no. 312 which was withdrawn in March 1958. The photograph shows no. 109 at Bridge Street in the livery that these vehicles bore when new. (C.Carter)

110   In 1955, no. 312 was experimentally fitted with USA made 'Earll' trolley retrievers, which were intended to arrest the wayward progress of the trolley booms following a dewirement. Although this idea was not perpetuated, the vehicle retained the equipment until withdrawal in 1958. This rear view of the vehicle at Haydock shows the trolley ropes and the spring loaded drums below the platform window. (E.K.Stretch, Omnibus Society collection)

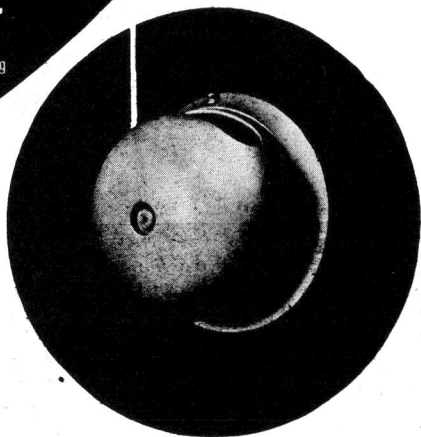

111.   **1950-1951**   **174 – 189**   **Sunbeam F4/BUT 9611T four wheel double deck**
Registration numbers: BDJ 74-BDJ 89

The post-war intake of new trolleybuses comprised sixteen vehicles, split equally between Sunbeam F4 and BUT 9611T chassis types. All had East Lancashire bodies of highbridge construction. The eight Sunbeams (with 55 seats) were built at the coachbuilder's Bridlington subsidiary, whilst the BUTs (with 56 seats) were dealt with at their main factory at Blackburn. As detailed earlier in the captions to photographs 55 and 56, special safety arrangements were provided to avoid these vehicles trying to negotiate the low bridges on the St Helens Junction route. The BUT vehicles, a type only coming into existence after the war, following the merging of the AEC and Leyland trolleybus interests, bore chassis numbers 001 to 008, although many of the type had already entered service elsewhere by 1950. Fleet numbers 174-189 were allocated so that these numbers were similar to the registration numbers. Fleet numbers 167 to 173 were never used. All these vehicles spent their whole lives working on the Prescot routes and were renumbered 374 to 389 in 1955. Upon withdrawal in 1958, all were sold for further service. The photograph shows Sunbeam no. 178 standing outside the Bridlington factory of East Lancashire Coachbuilders before delivery to St Helens. (Author's collection)

ILLUMINATIONS

112.   As noted previously in the caption to photograph no. 98, one of the original Garret vehicles, no. 2, was retained in the 1930s for use as an illuminated tableau. Its first appearance was for the 1935 Hospital Carnival, and the rear of this lavishly decorated vehicle is shown. No. 2 continued in this role until 1938. (G.S.Sandford collection)

FINALE

113.   Stanley King visited St Helens on the last Saturday of trolleybus operation, 28th June 1958. At Prescot he captured this view of, BUT trolleybus no. 388 being passed in Warrington Road by a Liverpool Corporation Leyland bus on service 10 to its home city. When motorbuses replaced the Liverpool trams in 1949, they had to operate a short distance along Warrington Road to turn round. Liverpool paid St Helens a small annual charge to compensate for any fares abstraction from the trolleybuses. (J.S.King)

114.   On the same day, BUT no. 384 has just arrived at the Market terminus of the Prescot routes on a no 11 journey from Portico, possibly, Stanley records, one of the last such journeys to be made. Note the difference in style between the two vehicles of the lower deck ventilation covers on the intermediate red band. (J.S.King)

115. The last day of public trolleybus operation was on Monday 30th June 1958, and on the following day, 1st July, a special 'Last Trolleybus' journey was made by civic leaders and invited guests using Sunbeam trolleybus no. 374. The participants are seen about to board the vehicle in Hall Street, with the depot building visible in the background. (J.S.King collection)

➜ 116. St Helens' Last Trolleybus is waved off by bus crews at the start of its journey around the no. 7 route. Above the vehicle can be seen the wiring and frogs leading into 'The Land' parking area on the right. (St Helens Reporter)

AFTERLIFE

117.   The eight Sunbeam F4s were sold to South Shields Corporation, where after some refurbishment, they entered service between 1958/9. As well as the provision of the standard South Shields destination layout, the rear upper deck emergency door, which in St Helens incorporated a platform for maintenance staff, was replaced with a conventional two-pane type. The bamboo trolley retrieval pole was slung above the nearside lower deck window in normal South Shields practice. They were numbered 201-203, 205-209 in the fleet, taking the numbers of withdrawn vehicles. No. 204, a pre-war Karrier, was still in the operational fleet, hence the gap in numbering. All lasted in service until shortly before the system closed in 1964. This view shows ex St Helens no 379 as South Shields no. 207, in the new owner's blue and primrose livery. It is seen in the early 1960s leaving the town centre en route to Tyne Dock. (A.Belton)

118.   Bradford took the eight BUT vehicles, and before entry into service there, they were thoroughly rebuilt, the bodies being dealt with by CH Roe of Leeds. The destination indicators were changed to Bradford's standard layout, and, as at South Shields, the rear emergency door was changed to a standard two pane layout. The front opening windows were taken out and the front panel was given chromium strip embellishments, plus a badge showing the city crest. They entered service during 1959 and were given fleet numbers 794–801. Many were withdrawn form 1964 onwards, but nos. 795 and 799 remained in the fleet until July 1971, having been in Bradford four years longer than they were in St Helens. Bradford no. 799 (formerly St Helens no. 387) is seen in the early 1960s leaving the city centre on a journey to Buttershaw, a route which, like most Bradford routes (and unlike those at St Helens), involved a considerable climb to reach the terminus. (J.Fozard)

119. On 21st June 1964, one of the ex St Helens trolleybuses, Bradford 801 (formerly St Helens no. 389) was hired by enthusiasts for a tour of the system. It was fitted with a St Helens trolleybus destination blind for the occasion and is seen here at Bradford Moor showing 'St Helens Junction', a destination that the vehicle could never have operated to in its home town. There is also a St Helens connection with the AEC motorbus seen overtaking no. 801. This was one of a large batch of vehicles bought in the early 1960s under the auspices of Bradford's new General Manager, John Wake. He had been in the same post at St Helens from 1952 until 1961, and had overseen the abandonment of the trolleybus system there. The destination layout of the motorbus is that introduced by Mr Wake at St Helens for the trolleybus replacement motorbuses, and he specified the same design at Bradford. (Author's collection)

120.   Upon withdrawal in July 1971, Bradford no. 799 was purchased for preservation and returned to St Helens for restoration and repainting in its original red and cream colours as no. 387. It operated at the Trolleybus Museum Sandtoft for several years (as shown here) and then returned for a period to the North West Museum of Transport based at the former St Helens trolleybus depot at Hall Street. It is currently at Sandtoft undergoing further restoration, and it is hoped that it will re-enter service there in due course as the only surviving vehicle of the trolleybus era in St Helens. (P.Watson)

MP Middleton Press

EVOLVING THE ULTIMATE RAIL ENCYCLOPEDIA

Easebourne Lane, Midhurst, West Suss
GU29 9AZ   Tel:01730 813169
email:info@middletonpress.co.u

ISBN PREFIXES - A-978 0 906520 B- 978 1 873793 C- 978 1 901706 D-978 1 904474 E - 978 1 906008 F - 978 1 908174

* BROCHURE AVAILABLE SHOWING RAILWAY ALBUMS AND NEW TITLES *

ORDER ONLINE - *PLEASE VISIT OUR WEBSITE* - www.middletonpress.co.u

TRAMWAY CLASSICS *Editor Robert J Harley*

Aldgate & Stepney Tramways to Hackney and West India Docks	B 70 1
Barnet & Finchley Tramways to Golders Green and Highgate	B 93 0
Bath Tramways Peter Davey and Paul Welland	B 86 2
Blackpool Tramways 1933-66 75 years of Streamliners Stephen Lockwood	E 34 5
Bournemouth & Poole Tramways Roy C Anderson	B 47 3
Brightons Tramways The Corporation's routes plus lines to Shoreham and to Rottingdean	B 02 2
Bristol's Tramways A massive system radiating to ten destinations Peter Davey	B 57 2
Burton & Ashby Tramways An often rural light railway Peter M White	C 51 2
Camberwell & West Norwood Trys including Herne Hill and Peckham Rye	B 22 0
Chester Tramways Barry M Marsden	E 04 8
Chesterfield Tramways a typical provincial system Barry Marsden	D 37 1
Clapham & Streatham Tramways including Tooting and Earlsfield J.Gent & J.Meredith	B 97 8
Croydons Tramways J.Gent & J.Meredith including Crystal Palace, Mitcham and Sutton	B 42 8
Derby Tramways a comprehensive city system Colin Barker	D 17 3
Dover's Tramways to River and Maxton	B 24 4
East Ham & West Ham Trys from Stratford and Ilford down to the docks	B 52 7
Edgware & Willesden Tramways including Sudbury, Paddington & Acton	C 18 5
Eltham & Woolwich Tramways	B 74 9
Embankment & Waterloo Trys including the fondly remembered Kingsway Subway	B 41 1
Enfield and Wood Green Tramways Dave Jones	C 03 1
Exeter & Taunton Tramways Two charming small systems J B Perkin	B 32 9
Fulwell - Home for Trams, Trolleys and Buses Professor Bryan Woodriff	D 11 1
Gosport & Horndean Tramways Martin Petch	B 92 3
Great Yarmouth Tramways A seaside pleasure trip Dave Mackley	D 13 5
Hammersmith & Hounslow Trys branches to Hanwell, Acton & Shepherds Bush	C 33 8
Hampstead & Highgate Trys from Tottenham Court Road and King's Cross Dave Jones	B 53 4
Hastings Tramways A sea front and rural ride	B 18 3
Holborn & Finsbury Trys Angel-Balls Pond Road - Moorgate - Bloomsbury	B 79 4
Huddersfield Tramways the original municipal system Stephen Lockwood	D 95 1
Hull Tramways Level crossings and bridges abound Paul Morfitt & Malcolm Wells	D 60 9
Ilford & Barking Tramways to Barkingside, Chadwell Heath and Beckton	B 61 9
Ilkeston & Glossop Tramways Barry M Marsden	D 40 1
Ipswich Tramways Colin Barker	E 55 0
Keighley Tramways & Trolleybuses Barry M Marsden	D 83 8
Kingston & Wimbledon Trys incl Hampton Court, Tooting & four routes from Kingston	B 56 5
Liverpool Tramways - 1 Eastern Routes	C 04 8
Liverpool Tramways - 2 Southern Routes	C 23 9
Liverpool Tramways - 3 Northern Routes A triliogy by Brian Martin	C 46 8
Llandudno & Colwyn Bay Tramways Stephen Lockwood	E 17 8
Lowestoft Tramways a seaside system David Mackley	E 74 1
Maidstone & Chatham Trys from Barming to Loose and from Strood to Rainham	B 40 4
Margate & Ramsgate Tramways including Broadstairs	C 52 9
North Kent Tramways including Bexley, Erith, Dartford, Gravesend and Sheerness	B 44 2
Norwich Tramways A popular system comprising ten main routes David Mackley	C 40 6
Nottinghamshire & Derbyshire Try including the Matlock Cable Tramway Barry M Marsden	D 53 1
Plymouth and Torquay Trys including Babbacombe Cliff Lift Roy Anderson	E 97 0
Portsmouth Tramways including Southsea Martin Petch	B 72 5

Reading Tramways Three routes - a comprehensive coverage Edgar Jordon	B 8
Scarborough Tramway including the Scarborough Cliff Lifts Barry M Marsden	E 1
Seaton & Eastbourne Tramways Attractive miniature lines	B 2
Shepherds Bush & Uxbridge Tramways including Ealing John C Gillham	C 2
Southend-on-Sea Tramways including the Pier Electric Railway	B 2
South London Tramways 1903-33 Wandsworth - Dartford	D
South London Tramways 1933-52 The Thames to Croydon	D
Southampton Tramways Martin Petch	B 3
Southwark & Deptford Tramways including the Old Kent Road	B 3
Stamford Hill Tramways including Stoke Newington and Liverpool Street	B 8
Thanets Tramways	B
Triumphant Tramways of England Stephen Lockwood **FULL COLOUR**	E 6
Twickenham & Kingston Trys extending to Richmond Bridge and Wimbledon	C 3
Victoria & Lambeth Tramways to Nine Elms, Brixton and Kennington	B 4
Waltham Cross & Edmonton Trys to Finsbury Park, Wood Green and Enfield	C 0
Walthamstow & Leyton Trys including Clapton, Chingford Hill and Woodford	B 6
Wandsworth & Battersea Trys from Hammersmith, Putney and Chelsea	B 6
York Tramways & Trolleybuses Barry M Marsden	D 8

TROLLEYBUSES *(all limp covers)*

Birmingham Trolleybuses ... David Harvey	E 1
Bournemouth Trolleybuses ... Malcolm N Pearce	C 1
Bradford Trolleybuses ... Stephen Lockwood	D 1
Brighton Trolleybuses ... Andrew Henbest	D 3
Cardiff Trolleybuses ... Stephen Lockwood	D 6
Chesterfield Trolleybuses ... Barry M Marsden	D 5
Croydon Trolleybuses ... Terry Russell	B 7
Darlington Trolleybuses ... Stephen Lockwood	D 3
Derby Trolleybuses ... Colin Barker	C 7
Doncaster Trolleybuses ... Colin Barker	E 9
Grimsby & Cleethorpes Trolleybuses ... Colin Barker	D 8
Hastings Trolleybuses ... Lyndon W Rowe	B 8
Huddersfield Trolleybuses ... Stephen Lockwood	C 9
Hull Trolleybuses ... Paul Morfitt and Malcolm Wells	D 2
Ipswich Trolleybuses ... Colin Barker	D 5
Maidstone Trolleybuses ... Robert J Harley	C 0
Manchester & Ashton Trolleybuses ... Stephen Lockwood	E73
Mexborough & Swinton Trolleybuses ... Colin Barker	E 3
Newcastle Trolleybuses ... Stephen Lockwood	D 7
Nottinghamshire & Derbyshire Trolleybuses ... Barry M Marsden	D 6
Portsmouth Trolleybuses ... Barry Cox	C 7
Reading Trolleybuses ... David Hall	C 0
Southend Trolleybuses ... Colin Barker	F 2
South Lancashire Trolleybuses ... Stephen Lockwood	F 3
South Shields Trolleybuses ... Stephen Lockwood	E 1
St. Helens Trolleybuses ... Stephen Lockwood	F 4
Tees-side Trolleybuses ... Stephen Lockwood	D 5
Wolverhampton Trolleybuses 1961-67 ... Graham Sidwell	D 8
Woolwich and Dartford Trolleybuses ... Robert J Harley	B 6